> "Silence is not the absence of something but the presence of everything"
>
> John Grossman

> "That everything will make you rich."
>
> Joshua Cartwright

Copyright Joshua Cartwright 2014
Living Words Ltd

2nd edition

No part of this book can be reproduced without express permission from the publisher.

Although this process has been used in the creation of millionaires, no responsibility can be accepted by Joshua Cartwright or his advisors for the accuracy of information contained in this book, or any action taken or not taken based on such information, nor can they be held responsible for any loss incurred as a result of decisions made by the reader. Specific advice should always be taken in each situation from an appropriate professional.

Table of Contents

Introduction: My Story 1
What is the Purpose of this book? 5
What is the Silence? 13
    What happens when you use the Silence? 16
Programming The Silence: The REPS(s) Process 18
    The REPS(s) Process in Detail 21
    Define Your Goals 21
    Creating Multiple Options - Link-Steps to Success 24
Relax and switch off your RAS 33
    Relaxation Induction: 35
EP – Emotionalised Programming 37
    Using Emotionalised Energy 38
    The YES process 43
    Permission 44
    The Art of KNOWING 46
The Silence: How to Access it 49
    Noticing the words in between your words 50
    Present Moment Awareness 52
    The Silence in the Gaps Exercise: What is your next thought going to be? 54
    Information Fasting 56
No-Mind: The Primary Exercise for Silence Training 58
    Extra tools 62
    Capturing ideas 63

Exercise: Super-focus 65

Switch the RAS back on 67

Seeing the pictures the Silence sends- learn Image
Streaming 72

Troubleshooting 74

Do you fear The Silence? 76

What are the benefits of The Silence? 83

Exercise: Turn on Your Genes, Turn off Your Stress 87

The Spiritual Benefits of Silence 88

The End of the Beginning 98

Sample Chapters of the e-book: FREE YOUR MIND
by Joshua Cartwright 102

About Joshua Cartwright 109

Appendix 111

Bibliography 123

Introduction: My Story

I know the secret of silence ... If we agitated souls were to understand the importance of silence, then half the troubles of the world will be solved ...

Mohandas K. Gandhi

> **In this book I am going to teach you how programming your mind with strong directed emotion and then sitting in absolute mental silence can make you rich.**

In my late thirties and early forties I really started to suffer from regular burnout. Whilst I was not (and am not) some high flying banker or stockbroker I had a four-hour commute to work and back, a bouncy, loving and totally hyperactive four-year-old, three teenagers living at home (brought from another country to live with us) a wife, lots of ambition - and lots of responsibilities. I'd made a lot of mistakes earlier in life and knew that I either worked to correct and conquer them – or give in to a life of mediocrity on low wages.

However, despite my increase in doing (working on several promising business projects at once) I was increasingly getting asthma attacks, silent migraines (where I got the dizziness and smell of burning but no pain) and sometimes I would just flip out in exhausted rage and shout at my wife and daughter.

It wasn't just that I wasn't getting enough rest: I wasn't getting enough downtime. I kept cramming more information, TV, and books into my head and expecting it to produce decent output. I had become addicted to doing and I wasn't prepared to give up any of my dream projects. (I am still not!) I needed a way to work smarter not just harder but I thought that the answer was just around the corner…in the next book.

Ironically, the start of my journey of using The Millionaire Silence began when I stumbled across the incredible *Bug Free Mind* books by Andy Shaw who taught me how mental control was the foundation of all of his not insignificant success. (He is a multi-millionaire). So I diligently practiced his 'no-mind' technique (which forms a foundational technique for The Silence).

I was able to quiet much of my mind and found a real sense of satisfaction in being able to push away distracting thoughts like never before.

However, I still felt overwhelmed and was still getting 'burn-outs'. By a stroke of luck or God-incidence I then met Ron G. Holland, the author of *Talk and Grow Rich*, and he taught me that The Millionaire Silence was actually where winning ideas came from; if I was prepared to 'let my brain do the work' then I could work smarter, not harder and take some of the pressure off.

As I started to use The Millionaire Silence (as directed by Ron) more and more I started to get some really great ideas AND to notice more benefits than just great ideas. I was calmer, gentler and more centered and my thinking was clearer.

I began investigating the role of Silence in science and religion and discovered that there are sound medical, philosophical and spiritual benefits to using it and, at that point, I decided to write this book for you.

You will be learning the R.E.P.S(s) process in order to generate ideas that will make you rich. If you have the faith to try it the rewards are profound. Yes, you can become financially wealthier than you ever thought possible but The Millionaire Silence will bring profit in **ALL** areas of your life. For this reason I'm going to refer to it as 'The Silence' from here.

> **Ron G. Holland has helped numerous people become millionaires USING THIS PROCESS.**
>
> **Get your 31-minute interview with him in which he shares more secrets of The Millionaire Silence***

If you are an innovator and/or an entrepreneur, _then you really need_ The Silence. The amount of information we are expected to absorb these days can be more efficiently utilized by _letting our brains do the work_.

If you are feeling harried, rushed - like you cannot stop - then this book is for you. You need The Silence. Every human being does; yet our society does not yet recognize the level of importance The Silence has for them. You have already found that the more you force your mind and the more pressure you put on it, the more it tends to gum up. So try something new.

To your highest and best

Joshua Cartwright

*To ensure you get your copy of the interview please email: Joshua-abraham@mail.com with proof of purchase of this book. I'll send you a Dropbox link. I'll also add your email address to a mailing list to let you know about updates and any other offers I think you would find useful. If you don't want emails from me, just let me know.

What is the Purpose of this book?

This silence, this moment, every moment, if it's genuinely inside you, brings what you need.

Mevlana Rumi

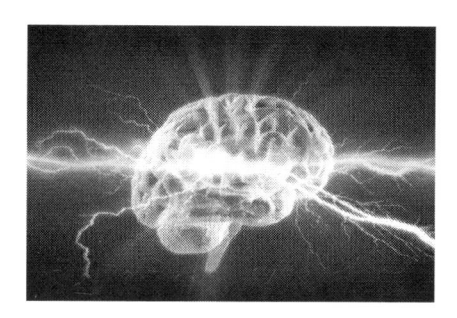

> Primarily, the purpose of this book is to enable you to access and use The Silence to generate incredible ideas for **bridging** the obstacles to achieving your dreams. These insights will show you HOW to get from where you are now to your goal; and the ideas you'll get will join the dots for you often in surprising ways.

Let's be honest here: this is one of THE main issues we face when we have decided what we want: *How are we going to get it?* If you are like me, you will have agonized over this question and often come up frustrated. Firstly, self-help books say:

"Set your goal then make a plan to achieve it". Duh! As if we couldn't work that out by ourselves. So what are our options at this point?

- Write out what we think will work.

- Research what others have done (always a good idea)

- Get a mentor or coach.

These are great things to do but the problem with them is that they are not tailored to you:

You still need to work out what YOU need to do.

And often you just don't know!

- How will I raise the money?

- How will I get those resources?

- I have so little time, what is going to work for me and for MY lifestyle?

- I feel stuck but don't know how to change and can't afford a coach

- And so on

Plus... as Ron G. Holland says, you need *hundreds and hundreds* of ideas across the lifetime of any big project or business.** If you have to generate them all through conventional methods (see note below) it can be very exhausting. Why not, as Ron says, 'let your brain do the work!'

So... In this book I am going to teach you two main things which I have learned myself:

1. How to program your unconscious mind and the Quantum field above it (The Silence) with your goals and link-steps (I will explain this concept)

2. How to access The Silence in order to get the missing 'links' in ***your*** chain of actions-to-success

I've called the process for using the Millionaire Silence: **The REPS(s) process** and I will be teaching you:

- R – How to **Relax** and switch off the Reticular Activating System

- EP – Set your goals and program your mind with **Emotionalised Programming**

- S – Tools for entering **The Silence**

- (s) **Switch** the Reticular Activating System back on

To be clear, there are other ways of generating new ideas *per se* (such as the techniques of lateral thinker Edward De Bono in *Serious Creativity* or *Six Thinking Hats* - or Roger von Oech's *A Whack on the Side of the Head*) and whilst I can personally say with confidence these are great <u>there is no guarantee the ideas will be right for *you*</u> **at that time**. The ideas produced by these methods are more akin to the results of brainstorming in that you may produce many stones but you then have to pick amongst them for the gems.

You have used The Silence accidentally to generate solutions. You've thought on or even agonized over a problem with emotional force then let it go, giving it up in annoyance or on purpose. Then later whilst bathing, walking, washing up or even making love the solution has popped into your head. Albert Einstein said his ideas came to him whilst playing the violin.

Sometimes the answer turns up in dreams. Elias Howe dreamt that he was captured by cannibals with spears that had holes in the tips. This was the breakthrough he needed to invent the sewing machine. (It also made him the second richest man in the USA)

Friedrich August Kekulé had several dreams of atoms dancing and linking to one another. After dreaming of a snake eating its tail he got the idea for the cyclic structure of benzene.

These are amazing stories but there is a way to get answers that is more under your control.

Using The Silence I can attest that **the solution generated will be tailored to your needs** at the time you receive the idea. (You still need to evaluate it but it will usually be obvious how relevant it is).

Some of the ideas you get will actually be **the** money making idea you need. In fact, please consider for a moment that *wealth comes from ideas* and one major aspect of creating wealth is the ability to producc ideas of value.

Sam Adeyemi, author of *Ideas Rule the World* says:

"Every human being is potentially wealthy and prosperous. The poor person is one who does not have ideas because ideas are the seeds that guarantee a future harvest. A mango seed is ultimately a mango forest."

In his book *How Rich People Think*, an analysis of dozens of millionaires, Steve Siebold bluntly states that the middle-classes exchange time for money whereas the rich-minded (what Steve calls the 'World Class') create leverage through **ideas that solve problems**. He says:

> "Every product or service that has made our lives better has come from creative thought. So when I say the world class thinks about how to make more money,

what they're actually thinking about is creative problem solving, not money itself. ... Money flows to great ideas like water. The secret is learning how to turn on the faucet."

> "Money never starts the idea; it is the idea that starts the money." - — William Cameron

As a result of using the process in this book I 'received' ideas for ecological power generation, new mobile phone accessories and shoe art (!) plus an idea for four brand new jewelry products.

I don't know anything about jewelry but these products are so original and yet easy to make I am currently working with a fashion house to get them into production. That's not to mention the massive increase in problem solving ability through the flashes of insight that come along with reinforcing my connection to The Silence. I regularly get numerous 'link-step' insights that help me towards my goals.

Please note The Silence DOES need to be programmed and this book will introduce you to how to do this. There will be work involved and because the self-help market is so saturated with books and techniques you may feel overwhelmed already with the programs you are trying to put into practice. Why would you want to add another one?

The simplest way I can put it at the moment is that using the Silence makes your mental machine run more smoothly, it's like a health elixir for the brain and mind. I am calmer, more focused and smarter since using the techniques in this book. There are numerous other benefits too.

So... to add incentive to use it I have also taken you on a little tour of history and science to point out how integral the Silence has been to the success of many great men and women. If they used it so confidently, you should consider it too.

I have included additional techniques from creativity pioneer Win Wenger and Ph.D professor Michael Hall which will help you receive the images and insights from the Silence more clearly – and even increase your IQ. Yes, there are techniques on the market that have been verified in independent research to increase your measurable intelligence!

We will also take a look at the health benefits and you may be surprised how good The Silence is for your wellbeing!

Whilst this is not a book on Manifestation *per se* it would be unfair of me to not point out that accessing The Silence *does* seem to speed up manifestation. The online ebook *The Complete Guide to Genius* claims that The Silence is a quantum super-position (a kind of ultimate place for manifesting) and repeatedly affirms how all great geniuses spent much time (if not most) in The Silence (without calling it that).

It's not my work so I cannot reproduce it here without permission but you will get fantastic, often original ideas, steps, actions and insights from this process - and these alone are often so cool you want to put them into practice ASAP.

I think there is some truth to some of the so called Law of Attraction material but as I am not an experienced writer in this area I will just point to a couple of interesting experiments that show your mind can affect physical reality.

Perform this experiment. It is easier to do in summer than winter and you shall soon see why...

Video of cloud bursting:

https://www.youtube.com/watch?v=1MsHXLbwkXE

or https://www.youtube.com/watch?v=fmj9kP6RQxA

You can also (allegedly) see the effects of different kinds of thoughts on water:

https://www.youtube.com/watch?v=tAvzsjcBtx8

https://www.youtube.com/watch?v=ujQAk9EM3xg

https://www.youtube.com/watch?v=PDW9Lqj8hmc

An interesting and relevant question is this: 'If your body is in fact 70% water then what effect is negative thinking having on it?'

(My apologies if these links have expired).

** Interestingly, Facebook founder Mark Zuckerberg explained to *Entrepreneur* magazine that he thinks big ideas are "...the result of a long process that involves solving smaller problems until you come across a bigger solution. It's not until you step back and look at the work you've done that you have that moment of realising what it is: When asked about the 'exact moment' that he came up with the idea for Facebook, Zuckerberg paused quizzically and said, "I don't think that's how the world works...Ideas typically do not just come to you," he said. "It's a lot of dots that you connect to make it so that you finally realise that you can potentially do something."*

So if you don't have your big idea now, this can motivate you to just keep solving smaller problems with the expectation that the bigger one will come.

*These dots are the 'input' that you feed your mind in the form of reading, visualizing and exploring possible solutions to your problem. More on this in a later chapter.

What is the Silence?

When a man knows the solitude of silence, and feels the joy of quietness, he is then free.

Buddha

The Silence is a mental-emotional-spiritual state of complete ... silence... mental inactivity: no noise, no pictures, and practically no feelings. It is not being like being dead but it is being completely aware and completely present with ...nothing...and yet everything.

You don't leave your body or astral plane or anything like that but you suddenly click or find yourself in a static yet moving state of quiet and profound alertness. Yes, like true love it is harder to explain than it is to experience.

Perhaps the quote from John Grossman truly says it best "Silence is not the absence of something but the *presence of everything*."

What is that everything? That's harder to answer (scientists don't know and philosophers guess!) but I *can* tell you (for the removal of comparison) what the Silence is not:

- **It is not relaxation**

Relaxation exercises reduce physiological arousal which reduces the chemical and electrical signals that cause 'rushing thoughts'. Sitting still, and calming your body help you get closer to the point of stopping your thoughts altogether.

- **It is not contemplation**

Contemplation is the practice of silently considering one's ideals (and other profound issues) in order to understand and connect with them more deeply. It is useful to slow down one's thinking activity if one's 'stream of thoughts' is especially rushing and busy.

- **It is not mindfulness**

Mindfulness is the practice of observing your own thoughts without judgment. It is essentially stepping back and watching and listening to what you think: which can facilitate greater self-awareness into what is going on 'in the back of your mind'. The famous Gestalt psychologist Fritz Pearl's stated 'awareness [of your thoughts] *per se* is curative' and I agree to the extent that, through observation, you can become aware of how your thoughts are creating your mood, behavior and mental health – and then work to change them. It also helps to prevent the 'snowballing' of thoughts and whilst it slows down mental activity, but it is not the same as mind emptiness or The Silence.

Mindlfulness can also be a useful entry point to The Silence as you can glimpse it in the 'gaps' in between thoughts. More on this in the exercises for accessing The Silence.

Fascinatingly, you cannot access The Silence with your thoughts. *The Complete Guide to Genius* says:

> "Controlling the mind to enter SILENCE is about NOT HAVING ANY THOUGHTS. It is the CONTROLLED ABSENCE of thinking which allows you to enter the Silence and nothing else. If you thought that you could "think" your way to genius, you are wrong.

You must STOP your thinking consciously and enter the silent state of mind for success to happen."

Where is the Silence? Over the last four hundred years' philosophers, theologians, and scientists have argued about what consciousness is and *where* it is. None agree, and as far as I can find out – science has not found out either. Even less so The Silence but, of course, there are theories.

Are we connected to some great energy matrix of conscious alla author Lynne McTaggert's idea of *The Field*? Are we receiving messages from God? Maybe, I am prepared to believe He is involved but I am not entirely sure what the balance is between our subconscious mind and Divine Inspiration. As this process can be used to generate ideas to be used for evil, perhaps there is more of our mind and less of Him?

I certainly don't believe the ideas of Socrates that we have all the answers already inside us. But when you use The Silence these ideas come from somewhere powerful - even if it just is your unconscious mind.

A last word for now from The Complete Guide to Genius:

> "Any genius, super successful person or anyone who has achieved anything great in life, was able to access a **SILENT STATE OF MIND**" [my bolding]

> This is what you will achieve if you practice and stick with it.

What happens when you use the Silence?

One of the better analogies I've found for how it might work is that of 'distributed computing'. This occurs when the unused processing-power of multiple internet-connected computers is employed in the service of solving massive scientific problems.

For example, PC's and Play-Station 3's around the world are being used by Stanford University to work - in their downtime - towards cures for diseases such as Alzheimer's, Parkinson's and cancer.

Basically, when your PC or console is idle the program on it connects to the project's master servers, grabs a bit of data and works on it until it has a result, which it then uploads. If enough of these 'spare cycles' are used then the hope is eventually there will be a scientific breakthrough.

In a similar way, when you learn to empty your mind your billions of mental connections go to work on the goals you have input and the steps you include to reach them – and when it has ideas it will release them to your consciousness.

It is just mind-blowing that when the ideas come they seem to come from...nowhere.... yet somewhere! It seems that when your mind is silent it is able to operate extremely powerfully and it is <u>extremely</u> active creating in that somewhere.

It's almost like The Silence pours a degreasing lubricant for mental cogs that have got gummed up by too much activity. Memory experts, such as Tony Buzan (the inventor of Mind

Mapping) have found that active recall of memorized information is at its highest ten minutes *after you stop doing any learning*!

Basically your mind is using the downtime to sort, connect and make the information you just learned more easily available to you. As we have approximately 86 billion neural connections that's a lot of organizing to do but your brain does it in ten minutes!

You will have experienced something like this when you have been thinking hard about a name you couldn't quite remember or some knotty problem… you give it a break in frustration and then later that day or the next day the name or solution pops into your head.

That's just a taste of what you can achieve when you program the Silence and access it on purpose except that the ideas that pop into your head will advance you towards your goals.

Programming The Silence: The REPS(s) Process

Ron G. Holland has written an entire book called *Millionaire Secrets* on programming what he called your 'billion dollar bio computer'. I have summarized his processes and added some additional trouble-shooting advice to help you make the most of the experience.

He compares the human mind to the Enigma machine which the Germans used to encode communications in World War Two and says that, when properly programmed, the mind will produce solutions to problems - like the Colossus machine (which was used to break the Enigma codes). This machine, way more primitive that your 86 billion brain cell brain, produced millions of solutions and helped the allies to win the Second World War.

This was what he said about the process you are about to learn:

> "By using the techniques revealed in this book you will be able to maximise your creative powers and money-making ideas, find solutions to your financial, career and relationship problems and achieve satisfaction, serenity and success in all those areas of your life in which it has so far eluded you.

... through careful study and application of the principles of Millionaire Secrets [and the Millionaire Silence] you will learn to create your very own "Eurekas On Demand" (EODs) thereby equipping yourself with a powerful and permanent capability to solve your problems and fulfil your personal desires and ambitions as they, and you, evolve and grow."

So again: What is The REPS(s) process:

- R - Relax and switch off the RAS
- EP - Emotionalised Programming
- S – Silence
- (s) Switch the RAS back on

(And just like reps of exercise, you need to keep doing this every day to build your mental muscles!)

Here is a fuller overview of the REPS(s) process:

1. Decide what you want and work out what it will be like when you already have it.

2. Create multiple options for attaining that goal – no matter how out of reach those options may be.

3. Switch off your RAS so you can program your mind directly (**Relax**)

4. Access massive emotion and program your mind – imagine the goal and the options being achieved whilst in a highly aroused emotional state (**Emotionalised Programming**)

5. Enter and use the Millionaire Silence as the mental womb for incubating and birthing ideas **(Silence)**

6. Switch the RAS back on to prevent accidental programming (**Switch**)

7. Receive the ideas

8. Take massive action to put your insights into action

I'll ensure you've got the tools to program your unconscious which will then talk to The Silence and produce the ideas you need. I've also included other tools which will increase your ability to program effectively and increase your intelligence overall.

As you can see, there are others steps that happen outside of the REPS process and I will talk about these as well. Now, onto the actual process itself.

The REPS(s) Process in Detail

Define Your Goals

First, define your overall goal and imagine it as a full-sensory experience:

You will need to have a goal/dream in mind (whether it be business or personal or both) but there are many books on the subject so I'm not going to linger on it. All I will say is that if you don't have a goal in mind you'll attain inner peace but not a lot else...

Although you can use the SMART goal setting process I recommend using the Neuro-Linguistic Programming Goal Setting Method as it is more thorough.

Answer the following questions.

> Please keep in mind that as you refine your goal whilst imagining it you should also refine your written version, add more steps etc. I do (as many others do) recommend writing it out as it creates a stronger neural connection with the goal:
>
> 'If you're interested in the biology behind writing's effect on our achievements, though, here's a little background: Writing stimulates a bunch of cells at the base of the brain called the **reticular activating system (RAS)**. The RAS acts as a filter for everything your brain needs to process, giving more importance to the stuff that you're actively focusing on at the moment—something that the physical act of writing brings to the forefront. In *Write It Down, Make It Happen*, author Henriette Anne Klauser says that "Writing triggers the RAS, which in turn sends a signal to the cerebral cortex: 'Wake up! Pay attention! Don't miss this detail!' Once you write down a

> goal, your brain will be working overtime to see you get it, and will alert you to the signs and signals that […] were there all along.'"
>
> http://lifehacker.com/5738093/why-you-learn-more-effectively-by-writing-than-typing
>
> As an interesting note: a psych professor at Dominican University of California found that people who wrote down their goals by hand, shared the goal with others and made themselves accountable for their goals were 33% more likely to achieve them than those who just verbally formulated goals.

So, here are the questions:

- What do you REALLY desire? [state as something in the positive that you *desire* rather than don't want]

- Why do you want it? And what is **that** answer you just gave important to you? Keep asking the question until you run out of answers or until you start repeating answers in different words. Those final answers are your highest values, write them down.

- How will you know you've got it? What will the evidence be?

- What will you see, hear and feel when you have it? Imagine you have already got it and you are looking out of your own eyes AS you imagine it.

- In which context will you have it? Work, home, adventure, professional?

- Who will be there with you?

- What steps will you take to get it? (Here, Programming the Silence differs from other goal setting methods so DO write down the steps you can think of but we will come back to this below.) Don't be concerned if you don't know all the steps – that is what this process is for!

- Do you have the resources to reach it? What resources do you already have? [This too is different so don't worry if you don't have all the resources you need.]

- How much of this is in your personal control? How many of these steps can you personally be responsible for actioning?

- Timescale: again, this differs so you can put something down but I'll teach you why 5 years or 15 months or whatever may not be the best answer.

Creating Multiple Options - Link-Steps to Success

One thing that **The Silence** can effectively provide is the missing links to getting the resources and solutions you need.

To do so, it needs as much information as you can provide it in order to generate solutions tailored to your situation. This is where you create multiple 'options' to success.

You can do this by brainstorming, using lateral thinking techniques (see books like *A Whack on the Side of the Head* or *Serious Creativity*), meeting with a mastermind group (a group of like-minded people) and generating ideas. I have even phoned up successful people and asked if they would mind me asking them some questions. Some have been very receptive to this!

Ron says he buys lots of Kindle books for a couple of dollars a time and reads them to study what successful people are doing. You can also do google keyword searches and look for authoritative information remembering that all that page ranks is not gold...! And don't forget your local library!

This approach is actually 'fast-tracking' your idea development by feeding your mind with lots of information to make connections that lead to insight. In the book *The Self-Made Billionaire Effect: How Extreme Producers Create Massive Value* x says:

> When we look at the circumstances through which so many self-made billionaires come up with the idea that snowballs into a blockbuster, we don't see a random and instantaneous flash out of nowhere, but instead a deliberate accumulation of knowledge and

experience acquired through a long-term commitment to a particular domain. Though there are some exceptions, the blockbuster idea is most often steeped in a set of skills or ideas that the billionaire has been immersed in for years— sometimes even decades.

You may be saying: "Hang on a moment – you promised us 'effortless idea creation' not years of working up to it.

Well, let's be clear, there is very little you can get for nothing. But I do not believe these billionaires had the benefit of knowing that if they pushed their minds with lots of input and potential solutions over a short period of time they might have come up with answers faster. You do.

Even so, as Sherlock Holmes said: 'I cannot make bricks without clay' and the intentional search for solutions that *could* be pathways to your success **is** the clay.

An example

You need dozens if not hundreds of potential routes however viable they seem. And - you must not let 'lack of money' be an excuse for dismissing any potential ideas. If, for example, you want to raise money you can and should include such ideas as:

- Placing an advert in multiple newspapers from tabloids such as *The Sun* in the UK) to broadsheets such as *The Financial Times*.

- Getting the banks to do searches for old wills and inheritances you might be entitled too.

- Get crowd-funding

- Go to innovation firms who pair designers with potential suppliers and distributors

- Rob a bank

- Find a business partner

- Ask family

- Invest in high risk stocks

- Accept an invitation from an African millionaire who needs to use your bank account!

- People just giving you donations or the money you need*

Yes, some of these ideas are ludicrous and stupid. Some are possibly too expensive for you right now. That is the point. But your mind can extract the best from them and still use them to generate your solutions.

Ron G. Holland also suggests listing every idea you can come up with <u>that you are sure *will not work.*</u> Why? Well, I think it's because your mind cannot process negatives and will actually use those ideas as references in its library of possibilities.

In other words, it's just more data for the creative powers of The Silence to work with.

Reading

Mark Cuban, the owner of the Dallas Mavericks credits his curiosity and appetite for information as the source of his success. He used to stay up till three or four in the morning reading about stamps and baseball cards. In fact, most billionaires credit reading, thinking about what they read with passion, and analyzing what they read as the source of much of their inspiration.

I unwittingly used this process some years ago when I became interested in a new form of psychology called Neurosemantics. The inventor of the field, Michael Hall, was putting out books on the subject but the information in them was not (in my opinion) well organized. However, I saw the potential of the field and craved to understand it. So I spent hours drawing mind-maps and trying to connect different pieces of information together.

His work did not provide me with all the solutions I wanted so I made a decision to invent my own techniques. To my surprise – because of my prior reading - I began getting ideas for psychological change techniques that were completely unique and which eventually became patterns in my book *The NLP/NS Users Toolkit* (available on Amazon or Smashwords.com)

One thing: I cannot tell you how quickly your ideas will show up but you must trust they will come.

Start from the final outcome to generate 'link-steps'

In *The Millionaire Inside* Paul McCormack suggests that you 'start by working backwards'.

> I have found that it many cases it's easier to list the steps backwards than to figure out the steps going forward. In my case, I knew number ten [he suggests creating ten steps at a time]: I would be a celebrity author, speaker and coach. That was "where" I wanted to be. So if that was step number ten, what had to

happen just before that? What would be step number nine, the step that would lead me directly into achieving step number ten? Are you beginning to see how it works? ... you keep going backwards until you get to where you are right now.

In Andrew Alexander's book: *I Am NOT A Millionaire: Mindset Shifts from Failure to Financial Freedom* he illustrates the process using the example of getting a fruit Snapple drink from the fridge:

> What is the FIRST thing you have to do in order to make that future a reality? The VERY first course of action you have to take in order to make that future real. I had to slide my chair back, and stand up. It can be that simple
>
> So by following this process, I had a thought in my mind (one possible future of an unlimited amount of pre-written futures), I stepped into that future, and I pulled it back and connected it with the present moment with that one action. The rest pretty much happened on autopilot.
>
> The key was paying attention to the details. The FEELINGS and EMOTIONS, the sights and sounds of being in that future make it real. Taking small steps back from that future and realizing what is the FIRST step you have to take in order to achieve that future. This allows you to believe that it is possible. (This is more important with larger goals outside of getting a Snapple). Yes, I know you are thinking that getting a soda from the fridge is not an example that proves anything. I did this for two reasons. The first, it is

these little, simplified successes that make it easiest to demonstrate AND practice the formula.

Secondly, it builds up to larger things when you want to set more long term results. You will learn how this process works for you by testing it. Perhaps the feelings and emotions aspect of the visualization works better for you than the sounds. Or the other way around. Fine tune your skills with these little things, so you have a higher success rate with the 'bigger' things.

Note: When you get more advanced with this technique, you will realize of your unlimited potential, and these 'bigger' things are actually just as easy as the smaller things when it comes to the level of work involved. I used this most recently by writing the first version of this book in less than a week. **I pictured what was possible, and then 'backtracked' to see what I needed to get done in order** to make it possible.

I should probably make clear again at this point that you are not expected to work out every detail for sure (although Alexander's technique seems to suggest that). Rather this is just another method of adding in link steps. You can (and should) have multiple

Intelligent Memory

Intelligent memory is where all the different processes for achieving solutions are held. For example, what if your earring (or cuff-link) rolls under a heavy sofa and you cannot reach it by hand? Do you just moan and complain or do you grab a coat hanger and try and hook it with that?

That is an example of using intelligent memory and although I cannot prove it scientifically I strongly believe that increasing the number of ways you solve problems helps The Silence produce ideas faster.

I say this because for years I had used lateral thinking techniques which, at their core, involve throwing together oddly matched ideas to generate entirely new ones.

This enabled me to make unique connections and improved my ability to cross-fertilize ideas from different domains to produce something new.

I recommend reading the book *Intelligent Memory* by Barry Gordon and Lisa Berger but I have also included the Random Entry technique by Edward De Bono (inventor of the term 'lateral thinking') as I think it very useful for increasing your ability to make those unique connections.

The Random Entry technique

Edward de Bono's Lateral Thinking tool, Random Entry, uses a randomly chosen word, picture, sound, or other stimulus to open new lines of thinking. This tool plays into the power of the human mind to find connections between seemingly unrelated things.

First, the person or group lists all the alternatives that they can think of without using the tool, Then they select a random word or other random stimulus. Then they juxtapose the stimulus alongside the focus topic and generate ideas to connect the two.

Here's an example: A law firm wants its lawyers to feel more relaxed and comfortable working long hours.

They take suggestions and alternatives from all of the lawyers and then pick a picture at random from a pile of photos to use as a stimulus for more ideas. They pick a picture of a bee. They then list ideas they connect their associations with bees to their focus.

Bees make a pleasant buzzing sound.

. There is an increase in the use of scientifically engineered harmonic tracks that affect brain function by slowing it down and making the listener more effective. Perhaps these tracks can be available to be played through office speakers to increase mental efficiency.

. Bees like bright colors. Perhaps letting the lawyers put up bright paintings that have two sides – a more serious corporate side on the other face that can be turned around when 'serious' clients arrive.

. Beeswax smells nice and some smells have positive personal associations. Perhaps arranging for scents that the lawyer likes the smell of to be available in his or her room after hours – for example: vanilla, baking bread or a perfume.

. How about having a sensory room with all of these things available?

Maybe these aren't the best ideas available but the practice of putting together connections will help you.

You may **also** now understand why creativity exercises like: Find 100 uses for a paperclip are so useful....! They increase your ability to generate diverse solutions.

Yes, it is a lot of work but think on these words of Andy Shaw, creator of the Bug Free Mind system and fan of Ron's work.

"The problem is, we don't think in the right way, as when we are regular travelers _we have programmed our minds to think about all of the stages_ to ensure we get to New York yet the first time we flew and for a few times after that we had to learn it.

So why do we assume that we do not have to program our minds for success when attending a seminar? Or anything else for that matter?" [my italics]

Ron says: "After you've done all the programming you'll find that 'success often comes in the back door'. In other words, it comes a completely different way you would expect.

---

*Just as a note both Ron and I have several times experienced people just rocking up and giving us money to do things we were visualizing as done. Whilst writing this book someone we had only met once before for a few minutes gave us nearly a thousand pounds to go on holiday.... I thank God for that!

Relax and switch off your RAS

The Reticular Activating System (RAS): You can see an image of its location below and note that it goes way **into** your brain. It is estimated to have 70 billion of your 100 billion or so brain cells so it's quite important to know the following:

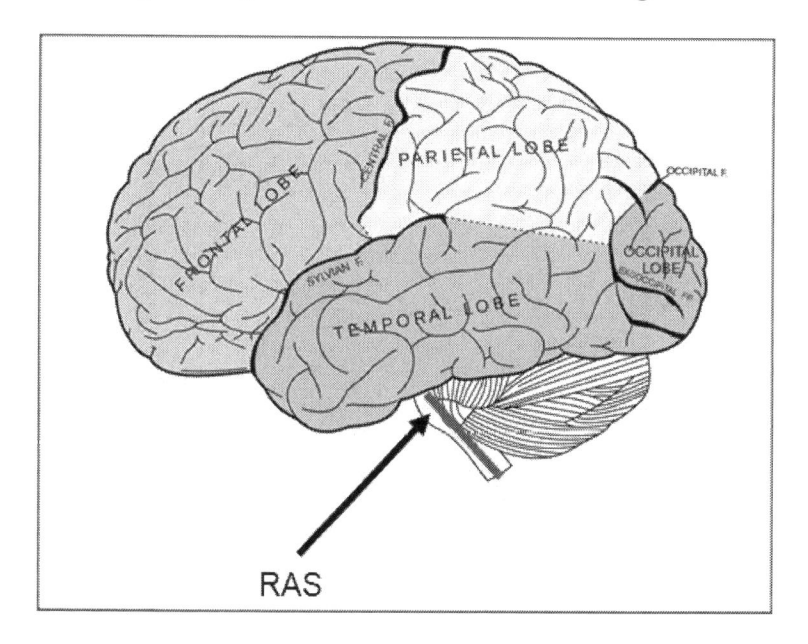

The RAS is a like a filter between your conscious and subconscious mind. It will filter *out* incoming information that is incongruent with what is already in your subconscious mind. This helps explain why you don't see the opportunities that others see – your mind is not programmed to see them. Therefore, they are not considered important by the mind.

(If your brain considered everything important you'd go mad with all the input!)

It's a clichéd example but it holds true that when you buy a new car (or more likely, a new smartphone these days) you start to notice when other people have the same type of phone.

Your new possession has been tagged as 'important' and thus your attention is drawn to it automatically.

What does this mean for programming The Silence?

It means that to ensure your instructions are not filtered out by the RAS *you need to turn it off*.

Then you can input your instructions (in the form of Emotionalized Programming) which, when accessing The Silence, will deepen their impact and help with the production of ideas.

(Note: the last step of this process is Switch the RAS back on! If you don't you can be extremely suggestible to negativity. This process is what stage hypnotists use to get people to accept they are chickens or have only three fingers!)

Here is a relaxation exercise. In his book *Turbo Success* Ron suggests you record it into your phone for up to five minutes. Some people may need ten minutes but over time, you'll start slipping into this deepest state just at the sound of your voice playing.

NOTE: I suggest saying before you start relaxing and when you are fully relaxed: 'I am now switching off my RAS for the purposes of programming my mind to produce the highest good for all'.

Use a slower, slightly slurred and singsong voice: the kind you would use when you are falling asleep and trying to talk.

Ensure you will not be disturbed.

Relaxation Induction:

> I am thinking of my legs and I am allowing my legs to relax. I am thinking of my arms and I am allowing my arms to relax. The more I think of my arms and legs the more pleasantly relaxed I become. I am now breathing deeper and deeper.
>
> The deeper I breathe the more pleasantly relaxed I become. As I relax I. slip into a deeper and deeper state of relaxation. My arms are getting heavy and my legs are getting heavy and the deeper I breathe the more pleasantly relaxed I become.
>
> My facial muscles are fully relaxed and so are the muscles around my eyes. The more I relax these muscles the more pleasantly relaxed I become. I notice my breathing getting heavier and my eyes getting heavier, I am now completely and utterly relaxed. My head is getting heavy, my arms are getting heavy and my breathing is getting deeper and deeper. I notice that I am very comfortable and very relaxed.
>
> My legs are now very heavy. My eyes are now very heavy. I have slipped into a very deep state of relaxation that covers the whole, of my body. I feel very relaxed and very comfortable. All the parts of my body are in a deep state of relaxation. This is an induction that you can experiment with. You can read this out over and over again onto an audio cassette tape. You may find that you need a five-minute induction to completely relax you. Others may need fifteen or twenty minutes. Find out what works for you. Remember you don't want to be asleep, just relaxed.

You need to do whatever works for you to get fully relaxed. If for some reason the above does not work for you I've put a couple more scripts in the Appendix at the back of the book.

NOTE: At the end of the session say: 'I am now switching my RAS back on.' Use a faster pace of speech and a more excited energetic tone of voice. Count from 1 – 5 and state that 'at the sound of the number FIVE I will be fully awake.'

A splash of very cold water will help as well!

So with that in mind, let's look towards programming your billion dollar bio-computer.

EP – Emotionalised Programming

"In Silence there is eloquence. Stop weaving and see how the pattern improves."

– Rumi

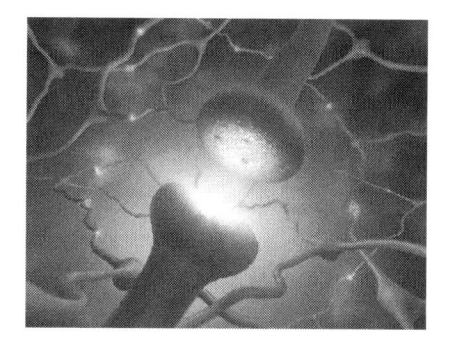

This will be the longest section but is one of the most important. You can go straight to the programming but I really recommend you read the following:

- I am assuming you have decided on what you want to have and have generated multiple options for getting it. This can be an on-going process by the way – I am still learning about finance and millionaire thinking as I go.

- You have overcome the first obstacle to programming by relaxing and deactivating your RAS. This is significant because your previous attempts at programming through visualization may have failed because your mind was blocking them.

Using Emotionalised Energy

Now, I hope it makes sense to say that your brain-mind runs on autopilot a lot of the time. It has too – you simply could not function if your brain-mind paid attention to every single new stimulus. It has to automate regular day-to-day activities like brushing your teeth or even driving to work (or <u>doing</u> your work if it is not that stimulating!)

Your mind only pays special attention to input when it is **highly energized**. And that energy comes from **emotions**. (I called them E-motions – energy in motion and in fact the French word for emotion means 'to move out').

The stronger the emotions the more your brain-mind will pay attention to it. Think of how fast a brain learns a phobia of spiders for instance. That jolt of emotion energy ensures that every time the person see what even *could* be an arachnid they freak out! That's powerful programming!

When your brain processes the energy it does so by firing chemical reactions in your neurons and repeated strong emotion binds the neurons together to form ganglia which then helps form neural pathways which can become habits. Your brain assumes by a law of repetition than anything you are repeatedly doing is important. It does <u>not</u> place a moral judgment on whether the activity is good or bad.

Thus if you have been doing something bad for you but do so with accompanying strong emotion (such as taking drugs) then you have an answer to 'How can it be wrong when it feels so right?' Yep. You've been fooled. It feels so right because <u>you</u> told your brain it is right. The fact that you are getting addicted, and ruining your life is not something your brain-mind will see as a problem until you consider it so This is the same for all habits from eating to pornography to weight-lifting (I couldn't think of something beginning with 'z').

This means that if you want to program your subconscious mind powerfully you will need to imagine having the things/experiences you want with **accompanying powerful emotions**. You will need to access the emotions or psyche yourself up to feel them.

(A basic knowledge of NLP and the inner representations called *Submodalities* can really help here and you can find the details in practically any NLP book – there are hundreds or online at any NLP site that offers teaching articles.)

So, assuming you know what you want you first need to:

- A) Imagine yourself having it **right now** – what are you seeing, hearing, and feeling, saying, and doing? See the moment through your own eyes as if you are actually there right now. What do you believe? How do these beliefs empower you to do what you are doing?

- B) Allow your emotions to get stronger and stronger as your experience the scenario in your head. Repetition or imagining turning up various elements of the experience helps here. For example, imagine there is are dials allowing you to turn the sound and colour intensity up and down (Submodalities)

- C) Keep running through the scenario making the emotion stronger and stronger each time. Really get into the positive emotion of the experience.

- D) Look around at the details, take note of how real it looks and feels. If you need help with this see the Reality Strategy exercise further down.

E) When you have imagined having the thing *as if now* you need to start 'experiencing' the steps and stages to getting it in the same way. I have given an example below.

You should adopt the posture, tone of voice and actions of a person who is experiencing the success he/she wants right now. When motivation experts talk about 'fake it till you make it' they mean that your body and mind use the same mental and physical pathways for fake joy as well as remembered joy (for instance).

So if you breathe as you would breathe when you feel joyful, use your joyful voice and walk with a joyful spring in your step (or whatever you do!) then you'll begin to feel it. If you're not sure what that would be like, find a role model or even a film character and position yourself to stand and breath and talk like them. Yes, this works!

Ron says he psyches himself up like an ancient warrior ready to go to battle. Yes, chest beating, chanting, anything to get the energy bursting through those neurons. You can also use the Yes process below.

Ron G. Holland has helped numerous people become millionaires USING THIS PROCESS.

Get your 31-minute interview with him in which he shares more secrets of The Silence.

*To ensure you get your copy of the interview please email: Joshua-abraham@mail.com with proof of purchase of this book. I'll send you a Dropbox link. I'll also add your email address to a mailing list to let you know about updates and any other offers I think you would find useful. If you don't want emails from me, just let me know.

Example of programming

I have designed a new range of jewelry. These are some of the many steps I am visualizing.

I imagine people wearing it in the street, smiling and happy.

I see it in jewelry shops and magazines. I even see celebrities wearing it.

I see and hear the top end of the range being bought in major London department stores.

I see the boxes arriving at the shops.

I see the items being packed in a factory in India.

I see workers making the items to the highest standards.

I see 400,000 in my bank account and that amount on my statement made up of multiple inputs of thousands: 5000, 15,000 etc.

I see my hand signing a contract and hear myself agreeing to supply 100,000 units

We have a professional photographer taking shots of women wearing the jewelry.

I ask local hair-shops to provide models. I hear women at church with the right kind of hair agreeing to model the jewelry.

I get the items made at shapeways.com, a 3D printing service.

I receive a donated cheque for thousands in order to get the designs made ready for factory production.

I see myself clicking the payment button.

I see and feel myself signing off the designs with the Spanish designer I am working with.

There are actually hundreds more steps along with this and breaking them down as much as possible is important.

The YES process

I have found the below helpful for when I am imagining and experiencing the scenario in my mind and body fully. It kind of 'seals the deal' and there are sound psychological reasons behind it working. It is a fast input of energy that tells the brain how important this is to you.

- Think of something that you can totally and utterly say YES! YES! I know what the obvious answer is but you could also ask yourself: 'If I could have anything in the world, what would it be?' and then ask: 'Would I want that?' Chances, are the resulting rush of energy with the YES will surprise you.

- What is your YES gesture? Your victory gesture? Do you punch the air, clap your hands, jump up and down? Do it, as you say your YES!

- Say your YES with as much passion and force as you can. Use Volume! Scream! Yes!, Yes! YES! And direct you attention to the most important parts of the imagining and visualization.

- Aim the YES and FIRE it (in your mind) at the desired car, the ideal husband/wife, the money. Trust me – it works!

Note: If you are someone who struggles to access strong emotion due to cultural beliefs or even trauma or abuse you may need to get professional help. There is no judgment here: only the fact that without strong emotion your results will not appear as fast as you want them too.

Permission

It may sound funny (funny peculiar, not funny 'ha-ha') but many of us do not have permission to feel our emotions. We have negated, repressed, and rejected the feeling of certain (usually 'negative' but sometimes 'positive') emotions* and will mentally do what it takes to avoid experiencing them.

In order to super-charge your neurons with enough emotion to attract/form images in The Silence you'll need permission to feel strong emotion.

This exercise involves giving yourself permission to *feel* these emotions - and deal with some of the objections your mind may throw at you. A full psychological treatment of what to do in every instance is beyond the scope of this book *but* I included the exercise because it is surprising in it's power to release of old emotional bonds and a greater scope of emotional flexibility.

(For further work on releasing emotions I do recommend the book *The One Thing Holding you back* by Ralph Cushnir as I have used it personally but as always, if you are depressed or on medication I would seek professional advice first.)

For example, suppose you want to feel strong joy about a new project you're involved in that is close to your heart:

- Go inside (focus your attention inside yourself) and say: 'I give myself permission to feel full and complete joy'

- Pay attention to the response. You may feel a shift as the emotion is released and flows through your body. If it feels at-all stuck give yourself permission again and ask: 'Where does this joy energy want to go?' (Thanks to

Silvia Goldman at Dragon Rising for this question) Let it go where it wants to go, no matter where

- Give yourself permission five more times.

- Adopt a voice that is both compassionate and will-not-be-argued with voice – the kind you perhaps would use to lovingly order a best friend to do something good for themselves.

Thanks to Professor Michael Hall of www.neurosemantics.com for this exercise.

*(I have worked with at least one person who overtly did not have permission to feel 'happy')

The Art of KNOWING

I was hesitant to include this thinking it might be too advanced but what the heck: you should know this process exists in your head and on paper.

I am presuming that you are convinced by the following:

- The sun will come up tomorrow
- Gravity works and is acting on you right now
- Your heart is beating

Think about each of those things in turn. What does it feel like to KNOW this is true? Not believe...let's leave believe out of it for now. TO KNOW with every aspect of your being.

Then compare this to something you *'believe'* is true. That you are going to wake up tomorrow. That you are a success. That you're the best (choose your talent) in the world.

How does it feel to 'believe' something?

Compare that with the feelings of KNOWING.

One is such a certainty you don't even have a doubt or a question. The other...hmmm...if you are truly honest you may notice thoughts in the back of your mind. At the least you'll realize that they don't feel the same.

Andy Shaw says that the difference between KNOWING and believing is that believing is doubting by default whereas KNOWING leads to creation and manifestation automatically.

I will give an example of this. A few years ago I decided to go to South America to surprise my stepdaughter for her birthday.

Although we did not have the funds in a flash I KNEW I was going. The money was found, and I went. A few years later my wife wanted to go – and again, we did not have the money. But we KNEW she was going and would not consider anything else. Three weeks before she went a couple we barely knew gave us a cheque for £1000 to bless us. Yes, we had to find a bit extra for food and so on but that was enough for her to go.

You can interpret this any way you want but for us we understand that the KNOWING – what religious people would call true faith – is creative. It helps to draw things to you. (So when you fear you have FAITH in something bad happening and the more convinced you are, the more likely it will be to happen. As Job said in the Old Testament thousands of years ago: "The thing I greatly feared has come upon me." Hmmm.

The reason I mention this is that if you can pump up that feeling of Knowing: immerse and soak yourself in the feeling and THEN think of something you desire but don't yet KNOW you are getting...the first feeling (if strong enough) will start to bleed into, envelop and become your dominant feelings for the second event. It's called Meta-Stating and the afore-mentioned Professor Hall discovered it.

- So...find something you KNOW is true.

- See, hear, feel and move whilst experiencing it. See a sunrise and ask yourself if you believe the sun is really there.

- Take that feeling and hold it in mind and body. It's hard to explain how to do this but you can do it.

- Think about the thing you want but imagine you are having it now. For example, it is so real I am standing on my houseboat in a South American river. I can see the river, the youngsters playing on the shore, the upper deck of the boat. I feel the cloying heat, see the Caymans swimming in the river, hear the cry of birds. KNOW that you have this too.

This will strengthen your imaginings and accelerate their manifestation.

Even more powerfully you can imagine HAVING HAD something. This means you experience the feelings of already owning a material item or HAVING HAD an experience.

For example, I desire to moor my houseboat outside my purpose-built house in South America.

So...I have already enjoyed walking around it in detail, seeing my family excited as they explore it and listening, watching and imitating the gnarly old boat captain as he taught me how to use it. I have seen it transported across the USA on a trailer-lorry (there are companies that do this), how it stopped traffic and had to have some telephone wires taken down. I have seen it loaded onto a cargo container freight ship which goes to the port of my destination and so on.

Do you understand how all of this is in the past tense? I am enjoying the feelings of HAVING owned it already. It can be 2 years ago or two weeks in my imagination. I am not sure it matters.

However, now my mind has to catch up in physical reality. The boat already exists for me.

The Silence: How to Access it

Now this gets even more exciting! The Silence is first and foremost a state of mind and each reader will vary in his or her ability to access it purposefully for the first time. To this end I have included a number of exercises to help you understand and experience it. There is nothing wrong with going straight to the main no-mind exercises – this is what I did – but then again I had previous experience of meditation which is not the same as The Silence – but a stepping stone to it.

If you have little or no experience of stilling your mind then I suggest working through the exercises from the start.

Accessing the Silence is a life-long journey rather than a destination. Yes, when you are fully in it you will feel like you have 'arrived' but to *keep* accessing it will take regular even daily practice.

The Silence can, technically, be accessed in most places: walking, showering etc, but this takes a high degree of self-control.

To start I recommend going into a room where you can be alone and sitting cross legged or in your favorite chair but, with practice, you can create the state whilst walking along a noisy street or running. It is even possible to create it whilst watching TV but as being in the state makes you more susceptible to negative (as well as positive) influences, I don't recommend it.

Exercises

The purpose of this exercise is to become aware of just how much internal dialogue is going on 'behind the scenes'.

Noticing the words in between your words

The exercise comes from the book *Words can change your Brain* by Andrew Newberg and Mark Robert Waldman. Be advised, it may feel strange even anxiety producing so, - if you feel such feelings - just take a step back from the emotions in your mind and tell yourself 'I'm just observing my thoughts and feelings like a scientist...what do I feel? What do I hear?'

All you have to do is say a single sentence aloud. As you do, *leave a pause of one second between each word.* Then say the sentence again but leave two seconds between each word. With each additional sentence stretch out the time another second. Notice how your inner speech reacts. Chance are, it will become noisy and agitated.

Here is the sentence:

AS YOU SPEAK THIS SLOWLY, NOTICE WHAT YOU EXPERIENCE BETWEEN EACH OF THESE WORDS.

Say the words slowly. Stretch out each syllable, each consonant. Pay attention to the experience of speaking slowly. Your mind will probably not like it and rush to fill the spaces with criticism and commentary on the exercise.

This is a sample of the kind of rushing stream of internal dialogue that is going on behind your conscious awareness. It is this dialogue we will have to stop in order to enter The Silence.

> As a side benefit:
>
> "When you speak super slowly, you'll begin to use the silences to carefully select the next word. You can actually think about what you want to say while you're saying it. In a matter of minutes, you may even begin to notice that you can communicate a great deal of information with half the words you would normally use."
>
> You may also find that a kind of peace descends upon your mind and your mood. It is not an essential exercise to enter The Silence but it sure has benefits worth pursuing. I now deliberately speak more slowly at work. At first it felt unnatural but my colleagues seemed to respond to it well and my communication is clearer and straighter to the point.

Present Moment Awareness

You will need to be in the present moment, the NOW to access the Silence.

Please consider that the only time we truly have is **now**. Tomorrow, even later today, is just another 'now' when you reach it. Yet because we can conceive of 'time' before now (memories) and also things that haven't happened or we haven't yet done then we can spend (and I do mean SPEND)! to many of our present moments worrying about what we did do and anxious about what could happen. For many of you, you may not spend much time conscious in the present moment...

So...answer these questions:

Q: Are you okay right now? Are you present right now? What is happening right now? Are you even here?

If you answer this question slowly - and come back to *now* your mind will quieten somewhat by default simply because you are not freaking out about the future or the past. If it tries to rush off again to some other place than NOW say 'Yes, but...am I alright now?'

If the answer is 'no, I am not alright' then **now** is the only place you can do something about it. Even if that doing something is deciding to ACCEPT it because you cannot do something about it.

Make sure if you answer 'no' that it is not a concern about the past or future trying to sneak in. Unless you are being attacked or harmed in some way - you are alright.

Yes, I know you have bills to pay and you had an argument with your partner and you overspent and ... but are you okay *right now*?

As you answer this and check your body and mind you'll eventually come to understand that if you do not feel okay it is because you are making yourself not feel okay.

If you have a situation, then you only have two options: to do something about it or to accept it. That will help tremendously towards being silent.

The Fist Clench

Clench your left fist hard for 30 seconds. After that time, take another 30 seconds to slowly unclench each finger watching them intently as you do. At the end of this time, you should be fully present or more present than you were. If you need to, repeat with the other fist.

How does it feel to be totally present?

My guess is it feels quite...powerful.

The Silence in the Gaps Exercise: What is your next thought going to be?

This exercise will help you become aware of The Silence gap **in-between your thoughts**. What you see meditating monks take years to achieve you can begin to benefit from in seconds!

Sit comfortably and close your eyes. Pay attention to your thoughts, just watch them come and go. Don't follow them, just observe like you are sitting, just observing.

After you've watched your thoughts for five to ten seconds, ask yourself the following question and then wait, in a very alert state, to see what happens immediately afterward. Here is the question: **Where will my next thought come from?**

What happened? Was there a short break in your thinking while you waited for the next thought? Did you notice a space — a kind of gap between the question and the new thought? Do it again...Yes... there it is.

Did you notice a slight hesitation in your thinking — a pause between thoughts? If you were alert immediately after you asked the question, you will have noticed that your mind was just waiting for something to happen.

At first, like Eckhart Tolle, the author of the Power of Now, says, this experience is like a cat watching a mouse hole. You are fully present, fully awake – *but there are no thoughts in the gaps...*

Watch the gap closely when it's there; look for it when it's not. Attention will expose the gap — the space between thoughts. *This gap is the source of thought – The Silence.* It may be fleeting, but it will be there. As you regularly become aware of this mental pause, it will begin to work its magic on you.

Please try the exercise again. Do it for two to three minutes with your eyes closed. Every 15 seconds or so, ask the original question or use a substitute such as: *What color will my next thought be?* Or *What will my next thought smell like?* The question isn't important, but paying attention is.

Once you are happy that you are experiencing glimpses, tastes and fuller moments of the gap-Silence you can move onto the primary exercise: No-Mind.

> **Main point: What is your next thought going to look like/sound like/smell like?**

Information Fasting

Okay gang, this is hard core. How about not being an info-zombie for a week (instead of shrieking for brains your brain shrieks for passive stimulation? Teenager version: Phone! PHONE! PHONE!!! I need IPHONE!)

No newspapers, no Facebook, Twitter, no personal emails, no watching Hula, Youtube, Netflix or Amazon or NowTV (insert your own visual crack dealer here). Basically, no technology time apart from answering phone calls.

Why would you even think of doing that?

Because... your mind is cluttered. And if you want it focused and able to produce more great ideas for you ... you need to cut it some slack.

How much do you really need to know about the uprising in Bolivia anyway? Or what Miley clothes-less is doing? Or which politician is outraged about this or that?

Do something beneficial instead. Access the Silence. Talk to your wife/boyfriend. Take a good look into the cat's eyes. Smell the roses. Feel the rain. Come alive again.

Unplug from The Matrix. You may become more Neo in a week than you think... It's a bit like giving up chocolate. After a few days you wonder what the hell you were doing eating it in the first place.

You will be giving up hours of negative programming. Don't be naïve...negativity sells. That's why I gave up watching soaps years ago (okay, except Grey's Anatomy!)

Try it...feel fresher and brighter. And get more ideas...faster!

Adam Boettiger, online marketing expert and author of Digital Ocean, recommends taking 'cyber-vacations'. "Every six months I take seven days to two weeks when I disconnect completely from the net and work with just a phone and voicemail," he says. "The whole idea is to unplug completely: it gets very stressful sucking on the information fire hose the whole time."

Thanks to *The OverThinkers Guide to Action* for this from the StartupBros.

No-Mind: The Primary Exercise for Silence Training

This is the primary exercise you will use to achieve The Silence and control of your mind. At first, it may be difficult to maintain even more than a few seconds (then again, maybe not). You are training your mind to be under YOUR CONTROL instead of letting it run you. This exercise is SO important that Andy Shaw, multi-millionaire attributes all of his success to having this as the foundation.

No-Mind, adapted from Andy Shaw's *Creating a Bug Free Mind* book

Shaw says:

> "On the path to riches, without control over your mind, you are simply doomed to repeating the mistakes you made in the past or merely mediocre success at best. If you do not master control over your mind, then there is no point in trying to obtain great wealth, as you will struggle forever until you recognise that this control is the very foundation that must be put in place to bring about everything else you study."

You really, really need to internalize what is said above. A lifetime of failure faces you if you do not. A lifetime of success beckons you if you do.

Your aim is to achieve at least 15 seconds of blank, empty mind, thought-less awareness. Your mind will need to be clear of all images, and sounds for that long ... and when you can do that... you must go beyond it. All great geniuses spend most of their time in the Silence.

- **Go to a quiet place*.** If you don't have one: find one or make one. Put the kids in front of the TV, bribe a teenager to watch the little ones, tell your room-mate you need ten minutes.

- **Sit down rather than lie down.** Later you will be able to do this standing up but your need to balance may distract you. Lying down, you may fall asleep.

- **Set a timer with an alarm** if you want to track your progress.

- **Clear your mind.** You will find the best way to do this yourself but imagining turning down the volume of the sounds and dissolving the pictures or sending them somewhere distant can work. Otherwise, just imagine a complete void.

- **Start the time**

- If you see a picture, start the fifteen seconds again

That's it. That's really it. It reads and sounds and looks extremely simple. It is...and it is not because most peoples' heads are filled with noise. In order to reach Genius level you're going to have to learn this to such an extent that you can walk down a busy street with your mind Silent.

I, the author, can do this more often than not after 18 months of training. But it won't take that long for you to get results because when you keep doing this exercise eventually your mind gets it.

If you have ever seen Super Nanny or any other such child-rearing program full of out of control 3 year olds then you will see that some have to be put on the naughty step 15-30 times before their little brain gives up because *they see they are not going to win*!

Your brain is like that toddler.

Please don't give up in disgust because when you stick with it the listed benefits (and more) will start to occur.

- Mental benefits: your inner chatter will decrease AND you can decrease it at will by re-accessing The Silence. This means that when THAT person is being extremely vexing at work – you can smile on the outside and calm your screams down on the inside. For real.

- You will eventually click into The Silence whilst doing the exercises. This is like, WHOH! Man. See Bill and Ted's Excellent Adventure movie for the reference! Awesome!

- People who empty their minds regularly suffer less mental illness than those who don't.

A word repeated from *The Complete Guide to Genius* may help: "The secret to success is to access the Silence **as much as possible**. What you need to realise is that your mindset doesn't achieve the Silence because you will sometimes have thoughts. You simply ACCESS it using your own mind." Very Zen. It will become clear.

Ron accesses the Silence in the morning and the evening. He is prepared to sit there for hours but not all our lives lend themselves to this! If you are self-employed you may have more time.

Personally, I access for about 15 minutes a day in the afternoon if I am at home and later in the evening. You can do more if you want. As you better you can grab 5 minutes here and there. Remember the analogy about distributed computing. When you access The Silence you're letting your mind's computing power go to work. Don't worry if it doesn't feel like anything is happening. Like Rex says in Toy Story 'Ya just gotta belieeeeve!'

But seriously. It is happening. And when the ideas pop out as you walk into that important business meeting you'll wish you had a pad.

Extra tools

I highly, highly recommend you invest in a pair of industrial headphones. These block out a lot of noise even if you live by yourself. They also give you a taste of real silence. I bought mine on Amazon.

If you have some expensive and effective noise cancelling headphones for music they 'may' do the trick but my ones are designed to create silence.

A stopwatch or timer is essential when you are training yourself to be Silent and you want to see your progress. Most smartphones have one or http://www.online-stopwatch.com/ is good for use on a PC or Mac.

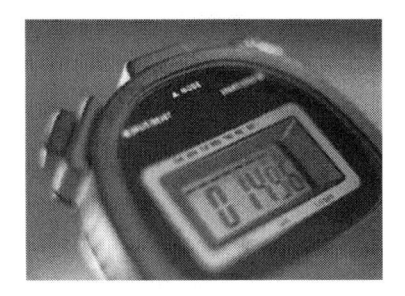

Capturing ideas

You might get ideas whilst accessing The Silence itself BUT YOU DON'T HAVE TO! This happens to me (the author) and I asked Ron whether we should continue in The Silence or 'awaken' and write them down. He says to write them down and then go back into The Silence. The truth is: once a good idea comes to my mind I cannot easily concentrate again until I write it down.

Because ideas can pop out at any time (walking, showering, having sex, going into a business meeting etc.) I recommend having a pen and paper on you at all times. I also speak into my smartphone voice recording function. Remember to play and write down the ideas later!

<u>Developing Ideas</u>

Once you have a solution you then have to test it out in reality. This is where you may need to do some extra work with The Silence because the ideas sometimes come in their purest form - meaning that you are given the *ideal* scenario of something working whereas the reality may need some customizing.

Let me give you an example: I am an inventor and I am working on prototyping some customizable hair jewelry. One piece of the jewelry needs to stick to another piece and be removable. I tried using magnetic paint but the paint was too thick and gloopy for such small pieces. It just dripped everywhere and spoiled the look of the piece.

So I asked The Silence to give me another solution. It came up with using tiny circular magnets which I bought and then found that whilst they worked well they made handling the little pieces too fiddly and awkward.

So I asked the Silence for another solution. It showed me a picture of Velcro but I have had to order some extra tiny Velcro as the standard Velcro you find on clothes is too big.

So each time The Silence presented me with a tailored solution that <u>absolutely does work</u> **but I need to find the corresponding real world equivalents to make the solution work in reality.**

Does that make sense? Of course, the ideas can also be simple enough to be instantly usable.

Exercise: Super-focus

> **"Nothing can add more power to your life than concentrating all of your energies on a limited set of targets."**
>
> Nido Qubein, speaker, author, philanthropist

Do you realize there is a direct link between you being able to concentrate and your ability to program and operate within The Silence?

For a moment...think about this logically...if you focus the sun's rays through a magnifying glass pretty soon you'll begin to burn the surface below. But if you move the lens all over the place then you'll diffuse the effect and make no mark. If your highly emotionalized consciousness is the laser and your ability to stay in the Silence is the lens, then your attention is focused in your subconscious mind and is 'burning' an impression.

In learning how to stay IN the silence you are keeping that lens steady and information will be able to pass both ways: TO your subconscious and FROM it.

The Complete Guide to Genius offers a primary exercise for developing awesome concentration, something it says is THE hallmark of true genius.

Again, the exercise seems simple but trust me, it is not.

Get a penny, dime, euro etc, and put it face down on a surface. Look at it, taking in the whole shape of the coin. Focus on the shape, not the detail.

Put your attention on the far side of the coin and gather your focus into one spot. Imagine you are mentally 'forcing' the coin to move. By this I mean imagine you are pushing your mental energy up against the far edge of the coin as you look across it, pushing as hard as you can. (The coin does not and is not expected to move for real!)

Keep your intense laser focus on this and push out any thoughts that try to intrude. You must do this for the exercise to work.

Do this for 15 minutes to half an hour. Yes, you read right. Genius takes sacrifice. Do this five days a week.

I started to see the results in about 8 days.

Your eyes may hurt after doing this and your head may ache. This is okay unless you feel it is not. You are eu-stressing your brain in a very unique and particular way.

You will see the benefits in how you concentrate on your everyday work. When you imagine your ideal scenarios and link-steps your focus will more easily stay inward.

Switch the RAS back on

This is utterly essential – make SURE you do this step. Remember, you turned it off so you would be susceptible to your programming. So turn it back on to ensure no-one and nothing else can make suggestions to you that will go deep!

Turn it back on by talking faster, dancing, drinking coffee. I slap myself around the face. No, I don't like it! You will know you are coming out of it when your fuge or relaxed state starts to wane and you feel more alert.

How will the insights come?

As I have previously written they can come at any time. As for their form it is likely they will come in one or more of your primary senses on the inside. In other words: you'll hear a voice, see a picture, get a strong feeling about something or a combination of any of these.

The prompt may come gently like a nudge or (as it does for me) you may sit up in bed and exclaim: 'Oh my goodness!' and then rush around like a mad person.

I really recommend reading the free book on Image Streaming I give the link for later. This unusual technique of describing your inner imagery forces your brain to search for relevant words and has the effect of not only making images clearer to your conscious mind but increasing your verbal fluency as well.

After several months of use your way of talking will be more sophisticated and there are verified increases in intelligence that come with this.

The main point really is: learn how your own insights come and be ready at any time.

> One last word: I was speaking to Ron recently and he said this about The Silence.
>
> "It took me a long time to figure this out but it is very profound. In the East they don't use no-mind for business and material possessions so the mind tends to gravitate towards the spiritual: peace of mind and that sort of thing.
>
> In the West I think it's imperative to link the no-mind to absolute specific goals…lead generation…books … Whatever your goal is. A lot of my visualization is revolving around those goals…a lot of what I shared with you about your jewelry business come out of no-mind….I know you want a boat… imagine that boat paid for…transported…really focus…write your statements as though it has already happened.
>
> I can't be clearer - I think it is absolutely crucial - unless you link it to specific goals it has nothing to work on … your billion-dollar bio computer…it will go towards spirituality."

You must 'own' your mind

Think about this for a moment: If you take full control of your mind it leads to full usage of The Silence.

And when you have full mental control you can program the Silence to produce ideas and implant your goals into the highest levels of reality you can access; then those clear desires will move down supercharge your values (if they align with them) and then affect your everyday behaviors.

Therefore, **You MUST make the decision that you are in control of your mind even if you are not yet.**

(This is a fundamental part of any successful endeavor – that you decide that you already have the thing you want before you have it. It is not enough to have it – you must utterly know that you DO have it. Yes, it is possible to have this state of mind even though circumstances and other thoughts seem to contradict it. See my book The Millionaire Knowing for more details.

It is the easiest and hardest decision you can make. You MUST decide that what you are thinking about IS reality.

Your mind will not want this, it will argue against it. Tell it to "'shut up, this is my life' and if I (as the Red Queen in Alice in Wonderland said) want to "believe six impossible things before breakfast" then I will. Muse on the fact that people believe the craziest things so if you want to be uber-successful in your mind then who's to stop you but you?

For me, the turning point was the realization that: "This is my life. If I don't decide this *now* then when? Do I want to wait another ten years?' At that point, I decided that what was in my head (the ideal life) WAS reality and the outside world was just catching up! I had to make a radical decision to adopt new thoughts and be serious about it.

If you don't want to take the aggressive route you can imagine what Buddha called 'writing on water' in that you imagine new thoughts are written on water and that they dissolved away almost immediately after they occur.

Dominant thinking occurs all the time...

According to Professor Hall *et al* your mind works by giving dominance to the thought at the top of your conscious awareness (and your unconscious mind dominates that thought but more on this below).

For example, if you shout at someone and feel guilty, then feel *angry* for feeling *guilty* and then *grin* at how *silly* all this is – the top emotion is humor and you will feel humorous about the other lower states.

- Humor @
- Silly @
- Anger @
- Guilt @

Shouting at person >>>>>

Sometimes these emotional states interact with each other to cancel each other out. For example, try being 'furiously funny' or 'angrily happy'. Can't do it, can you?

But…. You can always think ABOUT your previous thoughts. For example: think of a paper cup. What do you think about that? Probably not much. What is ABOVE THAT in importance? Probably most things unless you have a cup fetish!

Did you see how your language is the language of height? Just imagine for a minute that your thoughts stack up one above each other like the kids game one potato, two potato.

Your consciousness, the bit you talk to yourself in (if you do!) is the one at the top – the top potato. And the thought at the top…drives the lot!

So when you are thinking ABOUT all those other thoughts and make a strong decision to be in charge no matter what it takes you are thinking from the top of your stack of consciousness. There's a whole field dedicated to teaching you how this works and you can learn more at: www.neurosemantics.com or you can get my e-book called *Free Your Mind* which teaches a unique belief creation technique that uses the above theory.

The main point being though ...you can always have a thought about your previous thought meaning you can always be in charge of yourself... if you believe you can.

You must program your mind or someone else will. If you program The Silence on purpose you can expect it to reward you. If you let others program you (or the tv!) then you'll be led around by the nose. And that can hurt.

For more reading on this concept visit the introductory articles at www.neurosemantics.com

Seeing the pictures the Silence sends- learn Image Streaming

> Seeing pictures in your mind's eye is essential to being able to program The Silence for Maximum Effectiveness. So, if you 'don't see pictures this method will teach you how...and make your smarter!

In the 1970's two men (Richard Bandler and John Grinder who co-created Neuro-Linguistic Programming) figured out that we use the same senses internally as well as externally....

In other words, we get information from the world around us through our five senses: eyes, ears, mouth, nose and sense of touch AND in the same way we can reproduce the results of those senses inside of our minds.

This may seem like a 'duh' moment for those of you who can visualize pictures in your mind's eye but it might surprise you to know that not everyone can. In fact, predominantly visual people only form about 15% of the population.

Some people don't see the pictures but talk to themselves, some people predominantly 'feel' the answers (I don't know of any who taste or smell their mental conclusions...but you never know!)

As the brain predominantly communicates in images (which are there whether you think you can see them or not) it's helpful to bring them into awareness so you can see your ideas take shape.

Anyway...

If you don't see images in your mind it's extremely encouraging to learn that you can, and not only that – the method for doing so will verifiably help increase your intelligence. Researchers at the University of Minnesota found an increase of 1 IQ point for every hour of usage. Your verbal fluency will increase and your flashes of intuition will come faster.

Basically, you'll trust your mind more and more to provide for you the solutions that The Silence sends.

There is a free book at http://www.winwenger.com/ebooks/guaran.htm called *Two Guaranteed Ways to Increase your Intelligence.* It contains all you'll need to know to start Image Streaming.

Troubleshooting

Question: how long will it take me to attain Silence?

Research on those silencing their minds using yoga techniques (not taught here) shows that about 10% of novices experience complete mental silence the first time they try it. A further 20–30% experience being 'mostly' silent. That is, just one or two occasional thoughts separated by longer periods of silence. About 20– 30% experience being 'partially' silent, where the thoughts slow down and are separated by briefer periods of non-thought. The remainder experience a slowing of the thoughts.

Regardless of how much thinking activity decreased, meditators also report improved mood, decreased stress and tension, and an increased sense of calm and peacefulness. Don't worry if you didn't get there the first time, the main thing as the start is whether or not it felt good. I encourage you to keep trying. Our research shows that with every further attempt progressively more people get it. Most of people get it with a week or two of diligent daily practice…

My advice is whether or not you experience mental silence the first time you try, is to understand that it is a personal journey. Treat it as if it were a personal experiment: do it for 10 minutes twice a day for three weeks and then at the end of this time assess how you feel. If this routine is having a positive impact on any aspect of your life then continue on the journey.

You may not have realized this but, with practice, mental silence can be sustained even in the midst of intense activity, such as in sport, during creative pursuits such as music and art, or while enjoying the company of friends.

Q: Why is silence so important for the Silence?

Logically, this should not be hard to work out but to add some scientific meat to our experiential bones I'll just mention a couple of studies.

Scientists at the Air Force Research Laboratory in Ohio found that when two people talk at the same time, it degrades a person's ability to pick up important verbal cues.

In fact, practically any background conversation no matter where you are will interfere with your brain's ability to pick up important verbal cues or carry out mental tasks. Even hearing traffic noise in the background is enough to impair a person's ability to learn. This is why I recommend the headphones or even industrial disposable earplugs.

Q: What if I just can't turn off my inner dialogue?

I have experienced this for up to a week so I asked Ron what he thought. He said that in his experience if the mind excessively won't shut up it might actually be trying to tell you something. Shutting it down, in this instance, is not the best path to take. Go somewhere quiet, turn your attention inward and ask " What do you want to tell me/show me?"

Do you fear The Silence?

"Silence is only frightening to people who are compulsively verbalizing."

— William S. Burroughs

Henry Nouwen said, "In solitude, I get rid of my scaffolding." And what is scaffolding? It's the stuff we use to keep ourselves propped up, be it friends, family, TV, radio, books, job, technology, work, achievement, our bank account, etc

We are a society addicted to noise and motion. We live in a world that bombards us with incessant visual stimuli and noise. And it's easy to become addicted to such noise without even realizing it.

Many people of the tech generation cannot bear to be without some sort of noise, some sort of distraction. I was on the platform waiting to catch a train the other day and glanced down it to see *everyone* had a smart phone in front of their face.

My teenage son, at one point, started to physically shake if his phone vibrated while he was talking to me. If he could not look away he got anxious.

But all this stimulation comes with a cost. It leaves us...quite frankly...overstimulated and unable to relax.

I myself have experienced the other side of NOT getting downtime. I get nervous exhaustion, shout at my loved ones, and get depressed and fatalistic.

So visualize passionately – *and then do nothing.* Access the Silence.

We've had personal development gurus drumming it into our heads that we must take action, action, action. But frantic action without a plan is just thrashing around.

> "Take action by taking no action." Ancient Joshian proverb!!

Before all the beer-drinking couch dwellers start cheering about the above I should mention that you do NEED to take physical action, write, make calls, study etc.

Lack of Silence leads to lack of order

John Ortberg writes, "Hurry is not just a disordered schedule. Hurry is a disordered heart." You need order and focus in order to be able to benefit from the Silence.

We need to take this quote to heart:

> Emptiness is not our enemy. Everyone has an empty place. It is not something to struggle with or try to get rid of. Emptiness is part of being human. Emptiness is nothing more or less than a space within, a space calling us to find our own personal sanctuary. *Make friends with the empty part of life and find a vastness of peace instead.* Until we have stepped into the silent meadows and great valleys of our heart, a part of life will always be empty.
>
> The Huffington Post

When was the last time you were alone...with just your thoughts? Without the smart-phone? The TV? The tablet? The DAB radio?

There is a conversation going on in the back upper reaches of your mind **about** silence. About why you don't want to be silent. And you need to know what it is before you can reach The Silence. You have to know if not wanting to be quiet is just a habit...or a mental act of avoidance you need to stop.

Exercise 1

If you find that being Silent brings up emotions that make you uncomfortable, fear not! (Even if it's fear that you are feeling!) Ralph Cushnir author of *The One Thing Holding you Back* offers a way to release them AND free up emotional and mental energy. Sound good?

Well, you may not like the method but I can assure you it works most of the time. He says that you actually need to feel these emotions...because then they will flush *out* of your body like the passing clouds they were supposed to be rather than the rainclouds which pour every time you think about them.

So, in essence, here it is:

Go silent. Sit with yourself and attempt to silence your mind:

- What are the emotions that come up or try to come up and you are unwilling to feel?

- Notice how you are resisting feeling that emotion. Where are you resisting it in your body? Pushing it away? At which point in feeling it are you flinching?

What would you call this emotion?

- Ask yourself: What's the worst thing that could happen if I let myself feel and experience the silence?

Your mind may reply with pictures and words or just more feelings depending on how aware you are of your internal theatre of consciousness. This is okay.

If your mind gives you a scenario, then hold that in mind and ask:

- If this happened, what is the most awful feeling I'd have to endure?

If you don't get a scenario or answer, ask yourself: What's the worst possible version of this feeling I can endure? Imagine you have a volume control that can amplify your discomfort. Crank it up to the top.

As Cushnir says in his e-book: *The Mile*:

> Whether you feel it [the difficult feeling/emotion] in one particular spot or all over, stay connected to its physical manifestation. Whenever you lose your focus, patiently bring it back. Let your awareness remain soft and steady, without attempting to do anything.

Repeat as often as you need too.

The worst thing about doing this is that sometimes sitting with a particularly uncomfortable emotion makes you:

a) Want to run screaming from yourself

b) Wonder if it's actually going to work as the pain doesn't seem to be going.

Personally, the longest I have had to sit with an emotion is about 2.5 minutes. It just felt like longer.

But the feeling of relief afterwards is incredible. It's like you were emotionally constipated for years and just learned to live with the discomfort. Then you...what's a polite way to write this? ...found a release? ☺

If another feelings arises straight after this process, just do it again.

Exercise 2: Flushing out your meta-levels about Silence

This exercise exists due to the pioneering work of Professor Michael Hall and his Meta-States model. Thanks Michael!

Take a piece of paper and set it in front of you in portrait format. I strongly advise you to write this out rather than type it: many people swear it engages your brain more effectively than typing (he said, typing...hypocrite!)

At the bottom of the page in the middle write the word 'silence'.

Think about how you feel about being in silence. (Do actually be in silence whilst you do this!)

Answer this question: 'When I am in silence it means...'

About an inch (2.5 cm for you decimal babies) above 'silence' write your first answer of what it means.

Then ask yourself again and again, writing your next answer an inch to the left; the next an inch to the right, until you have a line of answers to the left and right of the middle one.

Then take one of those answers and ask: What does X (X = whatever this answer is) mean to me? Write your answer an inch above that. Then ask the same question of THAT answer – and write the answer an inch above that. Do this until you cannot think of any more answers or you start using words that basically mean the same thing – synonyms.

Then move onto the next 'bottom answer' and repeat the step above. And again until the whole page is filled and looks like the example below (with your own answers, of course)

What you just done is mapped out the hierarchy of meanings and beliefs that you have about silence. Some of your answers may shock you so it is important to be honest when you are writing them down.

For example, silence might mean 'I am alone' to you and 'I am alone' might mean 'fear' to you and fear might mean 'don't leave me' to you. Which as you will probably admit is not very logical but we are not talking about mathematical logic here, more the logic of the psyche – psycho-logics – as in psychological.

If it's in there, it's driving your thought processes and if it does not serve you, then it needs to go.

The next step is to take a break, at least ten minutes. Walk in the yard, have a smoothie or something. Actually, not the

When you come back to the page look over it and ask yourself: Which of these answers does not serve me?

When you find one or more ask yourself:

- 'What do I totally reject from my life? What would I never do?'

- When you have the answer, imagine yourself doing it fully (sorry, but it works!)

Take the rejecting, hating, spitting horrid feeling of NO and shout it at the page as you scrub out the answers with your pen. Keep doing so until you feel the hold of the words and concepts break inside you. It's like a little 'snap' then freedom.

NO!

What are the benefits of The Silence?

I've begun to realize that you can listen to silence and learn from it. It has a quality and a dimension all its own."

— Chaim Potok, The Chosen

Health

There is strong circumstantial (but not yet completely proven) scientific evidence to suggest that using The Silence actually causes the brain to rewire old thinking patterns caused by stress.

Researchers at Emory University found that suppressing thoughts can protect the brain "and reduce the cognitive decline associated with normal aging."

A team at Massachusetts General Hospital found, in a related experiment, that the repetition of personally meaningful words whilst in a deeply relaxed state could turn on certain stress reducing genes. (A version of this exercise is included below) The same researchers "suggested that similar practices, including various forms of meditation, repetitive prayer, yoga, tai chi, breathing exercises, progressive muscle relaxation, biofeedback, and guided imagery would have similar effects on our genes."

Even novices who had never practiced any form of meditation or relaxation strategy were able to alter their genetic expression in eight weeks.

The rewards are even greater for longer term mind-emptiers. Two researchers, Aftanas & Golosheykin, studied meditators using Sahaja yoga who had gone on to access mental emptiness/The Silence.

They found that the brains of experienced meditators 'had more theta and alpha activity than the novices, distributed evenly across the central parts of both the left and right frontal lobes.... In fact, there was a strong positive correlation between their ratings of happiness and the amount of theta activity in the midline of the brain across the two lobes.

Mind Inc, a company producing brainwave entrainment technology say "by learning to dominate the Theta mind state we can access and influence that powerful subconscious part of our mind that is normally inaccessible to our waking minds. While we are in the Theta state, the mind is capable of deep and profound learning, healing, and growth."

They also list the following as benefits of stimulating our brain with theta brain waves:

- Anxiety and stress reduction.
- Mind and body healing
- Immune system improvement
- Deep levels of relaxation.

Improved Emotional connection **with ourselves and others.**

Theta Brainwaves are associated with profound emotions. The interesting fact about this mental state is that as we deeply synchronize with Theta waves the intensity of our emotion increases. Sometimes when our emotions are blocked or hidden not allowing us to experience our natural emotions. By using Theta brainwaves stimulation through relaxation techniques or brainwave entrainment, we can return to feel and understand our emotions again and better.

- Increase in intuition

- Deeper connection with the subconscious mind

- High levels of creativity

Theta brainwave dominance is often found in highly creative individuals. Many talented artists, inventors, and thinkers are found to have been extremely higher than average levels of theta brainwaves. Utilizing the theta brainwave will definitely enhance your overall levels of creativity.

- Advanced problem solving skills

Have you ever suffered from writer's block? The problem associated with worry and stress is mind dominance of beta brainwaves, preventing to solve problems and get "mental blocks". Increasing your theta or alpha brainwaves will most likely help you reach the flow state without getting "stuck."

- Bridges the spiritual connection

Some people consider the theta brainwave the bridge between the physical body and the spiritual one. This mental state increases the feeling of peacefulness, bliss, and happiness. In fact, it's through theta brain waves that people achieve their strongest spiritual connection.

Subconscious mind programming

Theta brain wave stimulation enables you to access directly your subconscious mind. By doing so, you pass around your conscious mind that often acts as a "filter" and prevents you from changing your behavior patterns and negative thinking. In contrast, the subconscious mind blindly accepts any statement or affirmation that you give it, without question, and begin to act on it immediately. So, it's much easier to clear any negative thinking, thought patterns or attitudes that you may want to change, and to install new, desirable thinking and attitudes as part of your personal development and growth. In fact, this is the basis behind self-help techniques such as subliminal messages and hypnosis.

Paranormal Experiences

Increase of the learning ability

Though the alpha brainwave spectrum (8 – 12 Hz) has been associated with "super learning" abilities, the theta wave frequency range has been heavily related with learning skills. As your mind enters the theta range frequencies, you will be able to retain over 300% more information than you can while in the beta brainwave state. The theta wave state allows people to learn large amounts of information in a much quicker time than the beta brainwave state and may even be quicker than the alpha brainwave for some activities.

Improve long-term memory

Exercise: Turn on Your Genes, Turn off Your Stress

Sit in a comfortable chair and close your eyes. Take ten deep breaths as you relax every muscle in your body. Now repeat to yourself, silently or aloud, a word or short phrase that gives you a feeling of serenity, peacefulness, or joy.

Continue for ten to twenty minutes as you slowly breathe through your nose. Whenever a distracting thought or feeling intrudes, notice it without judgment and let it float away as you return to the repetition of your word.

When you finish, open your eyes and notice how you feel. After a few weeks of practice, you'll feel more relaxed and alert, less anxious and depressed. You may even find that you lose some of your desire to smoke, drink, or overeat.

Newberg, Andrew; Waldman, Mark Robert (2012-06-14). *Words Can Change Your Brain: 12 Conversation Strategies to Build Trust, Resolve Conflict, and Increase Intimacy* (pp. 32-33). Penguin Group US. Kindle Edition.

The Spiritual Benefits of Silence

Silence is extensively used as a spiritual method for listening to/hearing from God. I would like to take a look at this and other aspects of silence as it relates to the spiritual aspects of life. This is not an extensive review but I hope the wisdom and insights from these traditions can aid you in your spiritual journey.

I have no shame in admitting I have been a follower of Jesus Christ for 17 years. I am tired of the authors of self-help books pandering to the masses and being spiritually dishonest about what they believe in order to sell books. I am a Christian and I am open to the spiritual dimensions and benefits of silence.

I acknowledge that, for some, to mention the word 'spiritual' causes them to roll their eyes or the word 'religious' even more so. I am going to assume that if you are reading (and taking seriously) a book about a place where amazing ideas arise in a scientifically inexplicable (and possibly with the aid of divine help) way that you are mature enough to also have rejected knee-jerk labels and can think for yourself.

In other words, I am confident you will consider the merits of what some of the world's greatest teachers and their most devoted followers have said about silence.

You may rightly ask why I am including principles and quotes from religions whose major beliefs I do not agree with. The answer is: I deeply respect principled people who are ardently searching for their Creator and... their experiences and research crosses the boundaries of common human experience.

In other words, although I may not share the explanations and understanding of the divine being(s) they worship I do benefit from what their explorations and efforts to find Him have revealed when so much of it is conducted in and with silence.

Principle One

Whatever you believe or are seeking - Silence is essential to the exploration

Henri Nouwen, who taught at Harvard, Notre Dame and Yale (and who wrote 20 books) said "Without (silence and solitude) it is virtually impossible to live a spiritual life.".

The late Dallas Willard wrote (This one) [silence] is generally the most fundamental in the beginning of the spiritual life, and it must be returned to again and again as that life develops."

Austin Phelps, a pastor in the 1800s, believed that large growths in holiness "was ever gained by one who did not take time to be often long alone with God". He called this "an elemental principle of religion".

The Bible says: "Be still, and know that I am God." (Ps 46.10) with the clear implication that <u>stillness is essential to coming to KNOW God</u>.

Principle Two

Silence creates inner space to hear the voice of God.

God spoke to the prophet Elijah right after he had come from a power encounter with the Baal worshippers on Mount Carmel. He had fled because he heard that Queen Jezebel had placed a price on his head. He hid in a cave and God asked him what he was doing there.

Then God told him to leave the cave and that He would speak to him. Elijah saw a storm and then wind and then an earthquake and then fire. Yet God was not in any of those. Rather, God spoke in a gentle whisper (1 Kings 19.2).

Think about this next quote: it's very deep:

"The practice of silence ... its premises run very deep. They affirm the existence of a Reality that transcends space and time. Communicating with this Reality may look like isolation from reality when a person is not physically talking or listening to someone speak."

In this book we are mostly concentrating on use of The Silence for overtly practical purposes. But, as Pope Benedict XVI said "If God speaks to us even in silence, we in turn discover in silence the possibility of speaking with God and about God."

Principle Three

Silence in the Presence of the Divine is enables us to make better decisions

Before Jesus began his public ministry he spent 40 days alone, presumably in silence and solitude (Luke 4). During his ministry he withdrew regularly to 'lonely places to pray' (Luke 5:16) and seemingly did so:

A. Before making important decisions like choosing the 12 disciples (Luke 6)

B. To deal with grief (Matt 14:13) at the death of his cousin John the Baptist

C. To recharge (?) after performing miracles (Matt 14:23)

Interestingly, at His trial when he was accused he chose to remain silent. Given that He was fully human (as well as fully divine) at the same time one wonders if He had the strength to remain silent partly because of His training in silence. Just a thought.

Francis de Sales, who in the late 1500s developed sign language to teach the deaf about God, wrote: "There is no clock, no matter how good it may be, that doesn't need resetting and rewinding twice a day, once in the morning and once in the evening. ... In like manner, every morning and evening a man who really takes care of his heart must rewind it for God's service. ... Moreover, he must often reflect on his condition in order to reform and improve it. Finally, at least once a year, he must take it apart and examine every piece in detail, that is every affection and passion, in order to repair whatever defects there may be.

Silence gives us time to shake off the different pressures and ideas of the day that are contrary to our core values and help us reorient ourselves in the direction of the Divine we worship.

Here what the scriptures used by Jews, Christians and Muslims alike say:

"My soul, wait in silence for God only, for my hope is from Him. He only is my rock and my salvation, my stronghold; I shall not be shaken." (Ps 62.5-6)

If our minds are too hurried and full of internal chatter we may just follow what 'seems like a good idea at the time'.

In fact, Blaise Pascal, the scientist and Christian thinker of the 1600s, wrote, "I have discovered that all the unhappiness of men arises from one single fact that they are unable to stay quietly in their own room."

Dallas Willard suggests that the person who is capable of doing nothing might be capable of refraining from doing the wrong thing. **And then perhaps he or she would be better able to do the right thing.**

I have personally found myself less reactive and more willing to think things through even when I feel emotional. I can 'hold and process' for longer instead of just reacting. The spiritual principles I have learned come more easily to mind as well.

This 'pause of awareness' comes from an increased sense of consciousness and present tense awareness.

It allows us to disconnect from the world and deeply connect with our soul.

Principle Four

Silence is Spiritually Restorative

"For thus the Lord God, the Holy One of Israel, has said, 'In repentance and rest you shall be saved, in quietness and trust is your strength." (Is 30.15)

Moses and the apostle Paul, some of the most recognized figures in history, were transformed in times of extended solitude.

Silence and solitude is a tool God uses to restore our souls by breaking engagements with the world. It is really more of a state of heart than a place. Granted, it does include awayness from others, but as you mature, you can even be in a huge crowd and experience the rejuvenating power it offers. On the other hand, you can become a hermit and never experience its power.

We are usually surrounded by so much outer noise that it is hard to truly hear God when he is speaking to us. Silence and solitude frees us from life's preoccupations so we can hear God's voice. See the exercise on Information Fasting

Silence as not talking... as self-discipline

St Ignatius of Antioch, an early church leader said: "It is better for a man to be silent and be a Christian than to talk and not be one".

The Bible is full of praise for silence and many of the great Old Testament figures (Judith and Esther, Job and Amos, Isaiah and Jeremiah) talked about how pleased God is when people refrain from saying something ... because of their love for Him.

When Jesus Christ kept silent at his trial even though He was innocent His silence made a statement that is so loud it will be heard for all time.

There are similar sentiments in Islam: Imam Ali ibn Abi Talib (peace be upon him) says:

> He who speaks more commits more errors. He who commits more errors becomes shameless. He who is shameless will have less fear of Allah. He whose fear of Allah is less, his heart dies. He whose heart dies enters the fire. He who knows that his speech is also a part of his action speaks less except where he has some purpose."
>
> http://www.islamicinsights.com/religion/religion/silence-the-mark-of-a-believer.html

So not speaking can show your respect and love for the instigator of the spiritual tradition you follow. It is a way of obeying certain rules and submitting yourself to them.

King Solomon got his wisdom from God according to the Old Testament and in today's terms he was a multi-billionaire as well as the wisest man who ever lived. Wisdom is practical. Wisdom from the Divine is priceless.

Wisdom can come in the Silence

The Pope also said: "Silence is an integral element of communication; in its absence, words rich in content cannot exist. In silence, we are better able to listen to and understand ourselves; ideas come to birth and acquire depth; we understand with greater clarity what it is we want to say and what we expect from others; and we choose how to express ourselves."

He was talking about silent contemplation of the words of God in the bible

Speak less, be wiser

Nouwen wrote, "It is a good discipline to wonder in each new situation if people wouldn't be better served by our silence than by our words." (*The Way of the Heart*)

I was fascinated to learn about the Hindu practice of *mauna* the vow to remain silent as a method to cultivate inner serenity and silence within. It is practiced by spiritual leaders and ordinary people alike: at extremes some give up talking altogether, others limit themselves to a couple of hours a month or just communicating in writing.

http://www.hinduismtoday.com/modules/smartsection/item.php?itemid=4881

Mauna, to put it bluntly, can help us stay out of trouble. Chandrasekhar confessed, "I have committed many mistakes. I have been harsh to people and have hurt many with my speech. Finally, I realized the importance of silence. In *mauna*, the mind projects all of our faults. They come like flashes. We begin to look within and see our mistakes. This helps us to rectify ourselves. This can solve many of life's petty problems. The natural mind is filled with compassion and Divinity. I think *mauna* is the first step towards realizing God. It detaches us from worldly pleasures."

The biblical Proverb 10:19 says "When words are many sin is not absent but he who holds his tongue is wise."

Practicing Silence helps us control our tongue.

James 1.19 says, "My dear brothers, take note of this: Everyone should be quick to listen, slow to speak and slow to become angry."

Silence and solitude can free us from the tyranny we can hold over others with our words. When we are silent and yield to the advice in James, it becomes more difficult to manipulate and control the people and circumstances around us. When we practice silence, we lay down the weapons of words. It often reminds us that we don't need to say as much as we think we do. We find that God can manage situations just fine without our opinions on the subject.

Basically, if you mostly keep your mouth shut unless you have something useful to say, your life will have fewer troubles!

Silence restores energy

We have looked at the overt health benefits of Silence elsewhere in this book. But interestingly, read this quote from a Hindu scholar

"One of the foremost reasons to curtail conversation is to conserve energy. Abstinence from speech transmutes the creative energies of the mind in the same way that sexual abstinence, *brahmacharya,* transmutes the physical energies. Baba Hari Dass explains, "We talk only by exhalation. The more we talk, the more we have to exhale and the more life energy we lose. Energy is lost primarily in two ways--by sex and by talking.

The origin of both sound and sex is the *muladhara chakra* at the base of the spine. When we talk, we use tremendous energy. **This can be felt if you stop talking for a few days and then start talking again. The energy we preserve through silence can be used for meditation.""**

Isolation/Solitude forms an important part of connecting with the Divine

- Very early in the morning, while it was still dark, Jesus got up, left the house and went off to a solitary place, where he prayed. Mark 1:35

- After he had dismissed them, he went up on a mountainside by himself to pray. Later that night, he was there alone. Mathew 14:23

- At daybreak, Jesus went out to a solitary place. Luke 4:42

- But Jesus often withdrew to lonely places and prayed. Luke 5:16

Jesus went to places of extreme solitude. Yes, there would have been animals and birds and the winds. But His thoughts could be silent and he arranged his environment to connect with God and receive wisdom from Him.

This man and His disciples changed the course of human history. You may or may not agree or believe in what they did…but they did it. And it seems that being in silence was part of their success. The bigger part, of course, was that they were directed by God.

If you believe in God – how often do you listen to Him in silence? Or do you do all the talking? (I am very guilty of this!)

Silence is a spiritual necessity for you as a spiritual human being AND for accessing The Silence.

The End of the Beginning

You are now at the end of this book but only at the start of your journey using The Silence. If you are struggling, don't be concerned. Ron says that actually doing it, however badly, is part of the process. And anything you want to do well will probably have to be done 'badly' to start with.

If the mind-emptying methods in this book somehow don't work for you be assured, there are dozens of other mind-silencing exercises. Some are in the other books below, for example, *Silence Your Mind*, and others will be found on the internet. I picked these ones because I thought they were fairly simple.

To summarize the process once more:

1. Decide what you want in as much sensory detail as possible. It helps to work out WHY you want it too.

2. Relax, and tell yourself you are switching off your RAS for the time that you are programming your mind.

3. Imagine yourself HAVING the thing you want and HAVING HAD it – how does it feel to own/experience it and HAVE experienced it for some time?

4. Switch your RAS back on.

5. Enter the Silence for as long as you can manage. The more time you can spend there, the more your brain/mind will be 'processing' your request in conjunction with The Silence.

Go about your business! But be ready...the ideas are coming. [You can print this out on the next page]

Ron G. Holland has helped numerous people become millionaires USING THIS PROCESS.

Get your 31 minute interview **with him in which he shares more secrets of The Silence.**

---

*To ensure you get your copy of the interview please email: Joshua-abraham@mail.com with proof of purchase of this book. I'll send you a Dropbox link. I'll also add your email address to a mailing list to let you know about updates and any other offers I think you would find useful. If you don't want emails from me, just let me know.

THE MILLIONAIRE SILENCE REP(S) Process:

1. Decide what you want in as much sensory detail as possible (See-Hear-Feel). It helps to work out WHY you really want it too.

2. Use Relaxation methods then tell yourself you are switching off your RAS for the time that you are programming your mind.

3. Imagine yourself HAVING the thing you want and HAVING HAD it – how does it feel to own/experience it and HAVING experienced it for some time? Great, yes?

4. Switch your RAS back on. Speak faster, dance around, run on the spot.

5. Enter the Silence for as long as you can manage. The more time you can spend there, the more your brain/mind will be 'processing' your request in conjunction with The Silence.

6. Go about your business! But be ready...the ideas are coming. Keep a notepad or smartphone to hand.

A final thought...for now

The idea inside you may seem small at first but as you grow the idea in your imagination, what blossoms may amaze you.

It's your gift. Take that gift and grow it even more and share it with the world in a big way.

And the world in return will give you wealth and freedom and happiness.

From *The Millionaire Inside*, Paul McCormack

Sample Chapters of the e-book: **FREE YOUR MIND by Joshua Cartwright**

Reboot your Mind One Belief at a Time:

(Or... How the power of Yes and NO will revolutionize your life)

Will it? Will it really? You probably never thought that the directions you take in your life end up consisting of what you say 'yes' and what you say 'no' to.

For every thought or idea that has become a belief in your mind, it is there <u>because you said a special kind of 'YES' to it</u>. Either over time (as you gathered evidence for it) or sometimes instantly it became part of what is true for you about life (or some area of it).

Think about your convictions about what is right and wrong. Some you've inherited from your parents, you were told and shown examples of 'right' behavior that was drummed into you over the years. When you grew older you may have seen an injustice repeatedly committed and grown a conviction that this had to stop.

You may have had a 'lightning bolt' moment when you just *knew* something was so. It may have been an idea for a new invention, it may have been the bolt of love.

I went on one date with the woman who is now my wife and was struck with such a heavy conviction that she was for me, I never wavered from it.

In each case you said YES to something and it became your truth.

The mind lives on beliefs

We may have started life as a basically 'blank slate' but as time goes on it gets filled with beliefs about ourselves, our 'power' to operate in the world, time, other people and the world around us.

We operate out of and from our beliefs. What I just wrote back there is a belief about how we operate. There is no getting away from it. We live and work and love and hate and succeed and fail – through our beliefs.

Through what beliefs do you see yourself?

What ideas do you see others through?

Truly, as a man thinks in his mind, so he is. So be careful what you say 'yes' to – you might just get it.

In our early years we may have said YES unknowingly, later perhaps even carelessly. We were like babies who just opened our mouths (minds) and swallowed what we were told.

Over time we came to reinforce those YESES's and NO's.

We did this (and do this) because the mind tends to reinforce what you already believe. It looks for evidence to make us right in our own eyes. King Solomon of the Bible said this 3000 years ago. Nothing has really changed about humans since then.

Furthermore, what we believe is not just an intellectual experience, it is a felt one: we bring our thoughts into our bodies and act them out in word, emotion and deed.

We *feel* angry, *happy*, and most other emotions. We live, love, lie and lash out because our beliefs have become embodied and incorporated in our flesh. They *feel* real.

As a result it might never occur to us we could believe something... different. Maybe if someone suggests we do, we say: "Well it's all-right for you to believe that..."

Do you ever consider that there are 5 billion people on this planet and because many of them believe different things to you – *you might also be capable of believing something different?*

Interestingly, we sometimes don't consider changing our beliefs because we believe (!) to do so would be disloyal to the people who taught them to us. And what else would we believe? We can barely imagine it? (Read *The Awesome Power of Two Words* for help with this.)

But belief has changed the planet – and yes, often for the better. Jesus believed he had a message for all of humanity and because of Him we have the spiritual legacy of Christianity.

He said YES to telling the world that God wanted to be reunited with his children and now 2 billion people believe Him today.

Because of Robert Louis Stevenson we have steam locomotive power, because of Edison we have electric in every home, and because of Tesla we have radio.

Because of JFK we put a man on the moon, because of Florence Nightingale we have cleanliness standards in hospitals. Because of Steve Jobs we have Apple: and ipods and iphones and imacs (and all parents shout out "and IPAID!")

These men and women believed they had something to contribute to the world and were prepared to go after it. They said YES to their dreams.

But they had the same human frailties as you. Yes, they might constitutionally have had more energy or could survive on less sleep but fundamentally *they believed.*

Do you understand what it could mean to be able to change your beliefs about what you want and what you are capable of?

I cannot emphasise enough how your world changes when you realise that belief is perhaps all that stands between you and greatness.

What is your dream? What kind of thinking do you need to do in order to be able to pursue that dream?

What do you need to say YES to? What stupid, toxic, unwanted ideas about yourself do you need to say NO to?

With the techniques in the MetaYes and MetaNo patterns you hold in your hands the power to alter your destiny.

Is it really that powerful?

Yes!

Chapter 2 : Why change beliefs?

It's simple. If you want to reinvent yourself, you'll have to reinvent your beliefs. If you want to be more, do more and have more then it has to start with you *believing* you can be, do and have more.

The beliefs you hold right now determine your current perception of your reality. They don't determine reality itself as some will carelessly say. But your beliefs reflect what you believe to be true about life whether it really refers to something objectively true or not.

On a personal level we may have beliefs about our abilities that simply are not true. Physical damage aside we have much the same biological equipment as anyone else.

For example, I used to think I was 'bad' at mathematics. But basic mathematics is perhaps one of the easier subjects to learn because the rules stay the same and once you've learned the techniques for multiplication, addition, subtraction and division you just plug the numbers in and go. And I reasoned there was nothing wrong with my brain so eventually I figured out that it was my *belief* that I was a poor mathematician that kept me from trying!

What do you believe you are *no good at*? Does anything in life other than your *belief* in your inherent lack of ability point to this?

Your beliefs play a significant and determining part in how you will respond to life and what you will strive to achieve:

"Three generations of my family were on welfare, I'm going to make something of my life." (Said by Peter Daniels, a once 27-

year-old illiterate who is now one of the 400 richest men in the world.)

I can beat the four-minute mile threshold although everyone says it's impossible. (Roger Bannister: 3 mins 59.4 secs)

We must all kill ourselves before the authorities get to us. (Jim Jones, 1978, JonesTown, Guyana – site of the mass suicide of nearly 1000 people including children.)

What could you be missing out on? What could you really achieve if you believed you could? There's a world of difference between a real can't and a psychological can't.

Real can'ts (although in ten years I could be wrong ☺ !!)

- You can't jump off the Chrysler Building unaided and survive.
- You can't teleport yourself to China.
- You can't look two ways at once.

Psychological Can't (may not be true)

- I can't do/learn/master X(e.g. mathematics, ballroom dancing, case law principles, memorising dates, plumbing etc)
- I can't talk to that man/woman/girl/boy I like
- I have a problem managing my money

You'll be able to use the Meta-No Pattern to get rid of those psychological can'ts and start creating some more useful can-do's.

If you enjoyed this sample please visit my book page on Amazon.

About Joshua Cartwright

Joshua Cartwright is the author of eight books and over 130 articles on personal development.

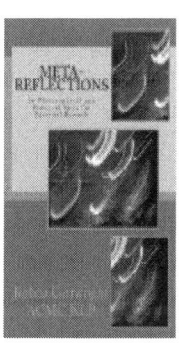

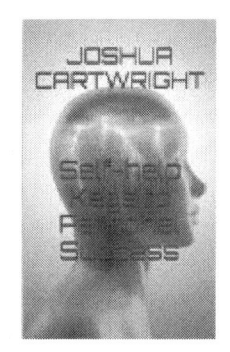

To your highest and best

Joshua & Glenda Cartwright

Appendix

If you are having trouble relaxing: Record this scripts on a phone or PC/MAC and play them back to yourself whilst relaxing. Your own voice has a lot of authority in your own life. Then go onto use Emotionalised Programming.

Method 1

You can close your eyes now ... And begin breathing deeply and slowly ... Before you let go completely, and go into a deep hypnotic state, just let yourself listen carefully to everything I say to you ... It's going to happen automatically ... So you don't need to think about that now ... And you will need no conscious control over what happens ... The muscles in and around your eyes will relax all by themselves as you continue breathing ... Easily and freely ... Without thinking about it, you will soon enter a deep, peaceful, relaxed sort of situation without any effort ... There is nothing important for your conscious mind to do... absolutely nothing whatsoever to do except to relax... There is nothing really important except the activities of your subconscious mind ... And that can be just as automatic as dreaming ... And you know how easily you can forget your dreams when you awaken ... You are already drifting into this relaxed state of hypnosis... Without noticing it, you have already altered your rate of breathing ... You are breathing much more easily and freely... and yet you had not thought about your breathing except at the beginning...

And now you can really enjoy relaxing more and more, and your subconscious mind will listen to each word I say ... And it keeps becoming less important for you to consciously listen to my voice ... Your subconscious mind can hear even if I whisper ... You are continuing to drift into a more detached state as you examine privately in your own mind ... Secrets, feelings, sensations, and behavior you didn't know you had ... At the same time, letting go completely ... Your own mind is solving that problem ... At your own pace ... Just as rapidly as it feels you are ready ... You continue becoming more relaxed and comfortable as you sit there with your eyes closed ... As you experience that deepening comfort you don't have to move, or talk, or let anything bother you ... Your own inner mind can respond automatically to everything I tell you ... and you will be pleasantly surprised with your continuous progress ...

You are getting much closer to a deep hypnotic trance ... And you are beginning to realize that you don't care whether or not you are going into a deep trance ... Being in this peaceful state enables you to experience the comfort of the hypnotic trance ... Being hypnotized is always a very enjoyable, very pleasant, calm, peaceful, completely relaxing experience ... It seems natural ... to include hypnosis in your future ... either self-hypnosis... or having someone hypnotise you...You will always enjoy the sensations ... Of comfort ... Of calmness ... And all the other sensations that come automatically from this wonderful experience ... You will find yourself feeling really happy that you have now discovered hypnosis... discovered hypnosis and all the positive benefits that it can mean for you... Because you are learning something about yourself ... You are developing your own techniques of therapy ... Without knowing you are developing them ...You can have it as a surprise sooner or later ... a very pleasant surprise ... Imagine yourself in a place you like very much ... By a lake, or by the ocean ... Perhaps you are floating gently on a sailboat on a peaceful lake ... On a warm, summer day ... You are continuing to relax even more now ... And you continue becoming more comfortable ... This is your own world that you like very much ... You are going to find that any time you want to spend a few minutes by yourself, relaxing, and feeling very comfortable and serene, you can automatically go back to this feeling you're experiencing now ... You can put yourself into this world anytime you like ... There are times when you will want this serene feeling ... And it is yours whenever you want it ...

Continue enjoying this pleasant experience as your subconscious mind is receiving everything I tell you ... And you will be pleased at the way you automatically respond to everything I say.

Method 2

First, be sure that you will not be disturbed.

Second, remove your shoes or any apparel that will interfere with your physical comfort in any way.

Third, now stretch out on your back, with your legs separated, so that no part of your calves or thighs are touching. Keep feet separated at least 8 to 10 inches; arms extended loosely and limply alongside your body, palms facing downward and fingers limply outstretched.

Once we begin, you can help by remaining quiet and passive. Our first goal is for you to become unaware of your body. You can best achieve that goal by avoiding movement. The first thing that I want you to do is to fix your eyes at a spot on the ceiling overhead. Pick out an imaginary spot, and stare at that spot without moving a muscle.

Now, take a deep breath and fill up your lungs. Exhale slowly. Sleep now. Now, take a second and even deeper breath. Take in all the air that your lungs can hold. Exhale slowly. Sleep now. Now, let your eyelids close down. Now, your eyelids are closed down. Please leave them closed down until I ask you to open them again. You will always be able to open your eyes, unless I were to give you a direct command and tell you that your eyelids are locked closed. And I don't intend to do that. Hypnosis is a state of mind, not a state of eyelids. Now, I want you to mentally picture and imagine that you are looking at the muscles in the tips of the toes of your left foot. In your imagination, follow those muscles as they move back into the ball of the foot. In your imagination, follow those muscles as they move back into the ball of the foot. Back into the arch, and all the way back into the heel. Now, turn all those muscles loose. Let them grow limp and lazy, just like a handful of loose rubber bands.

Now, as the muscles begin to relax, just let your mind relax, too. Let your mind drift where it will. Let your mind drift off to pleasant scenes in your imagination. And now, let the relaxation move on up, into the ankle now. From the ankle, all the way up to the left knee. The calf muscles begin to grow loose and limp -- heavy, and so relaxed. All of your tensions are fading away. You're relaxing more with each easy breath that you take. Begin breathing more deeply, now, just as you breathe each night, when you are deep and sound in slumber. Just imagine that you can see your breath as a white mist, coming from your nostrils. Each and every time that you exhale this white mist, you are freeing yourself of tension, and going deeper, deeper into drowsy relaxation. Now, from the knee, all the way to the left hip, the long thigh muscles are turning loose, easing off, and just relaxing now. Now, as those muscles relax, just let go a little more, and gently, calmly, easily, drift on over, into a pleasant state of easy relaxation.

Now let the wave of relaxation that started from the toes of your left foot just a few seconds ago -- let it move over now into the toes of the right foot, back into the arch, and all the way back to the heel. Turn all of those muscles loose, and go deeper and deeper into relaxation. Into the ankle, the muscles let go. From the ankle, all the way up to the right knee. The calf muscles are turning loose and letting go. You're relaxing more with each easy breath that you take. With each sound that you hear. Each sound carries you deeper, deeper and sounder in sleep. From the knee, all the way up to the right hip. The long thigh muscles grow limp and lazy. Now, as those muscles relax, just go all the way down, deeper and deeper in drowsy slumber. Turn them all loose and go deeper in sleep.

Now, the wave of relaxation moves on up, into the stomach now. Into the solar plexus, the center of nervous energy. Each muscle and nerve lets loose the tensions, relaxing. You're drifting down, deeper and deeper in sleep. Down, deeper in slumber. Up through the ribs, the muscles relax. Into the broad muscles of the chest. The muscles of the chest grow limp and loose, and so relaxed. All of your tensions are fading away. You're relaxing now, more with each easy beat of your heart, and going deeper in drowsy slumber. Into the neck, the muscles let go. All around the neck, the muscles relax, just as they relax each night when you are deep and sound in sleep. Turn them all loose, and go deeper and deeper in slumber. Now let the relaxation start down your back. From the base of the skull to the base of the spine. Each muscle and nerve along the spine lets loose the tension, relaxing, your drifting down. Deeper and deeper in sleep. down deeper in drowsy slumber. And the wave of relaxation spreads out into the broad muscles of the back.

Now all across the small of the back. All across the back of the shoulders. Turn loose every muscle and every nerve in the back, and go deeper and deeper in sleep. Into the shoulder, the muscles let go. From the shoulders, down to the elbows of both arms. The upper arm muscles are turning loose, easing off, and just relaxing now. From the elbows, down to the wrists on both arms, the forearm muscles grow limp and lazy. From the wrists to the fingertips of both hands, each muscle and nerve lets loose the tensions, relaxing, you're drifting down. Deeper and deeper in sleep. Into the jaws, the muscles relax. The jaws are parting slightly, teeth not quite touching. All around the mouth, the muscles let go. Up through the nose, each nerve gives way. All around the eyes, the muscles are heavy, and so relaxed. Even your eyebrows are relaxing now. Across the forehead, the muscles smooth out. Across the top of the skull.

Down the back of the neck. Down through the temples, back around the ears, all of the muscles are loose, and lazy -- just like a handful of loose rubber bands.

And you may feel now, a pleasant tingling sensation in the tips of your toes, or in your fingertips -- a pleasant tingling sensation, growing stronger and stronger now, as your entire body is being bathed in the pleasant glow of complete and utter relaxation.

Now you are completely relaxed. Each muscle and nerve in your body is loose and limp and relaxed, and you feel good.

Method 3

I've found this to be a very good script for dealing with the hyper-vigilant individual or the particularly analytical type of personality. It is extremely permissive but at the same time, almost impossible to resist.

Ok, just make yourself comfortable now... if you want to close your eyes, that's a good idea, but if you don't, that's fine too... now you can just listen quietly to the sound of my voice... and of course you'll be aware of all those other sounds, too.... sounds inside the building, sounds from outside... but these won't disturb you... In fact they are going to help to relax you, because the only sound you need to think about is the sound of my voice... and while you're listening to the sound of my voice you can just simply allow yourself to be as lazy as you could ever want to be.... Just allow yourself to be as lazy as you could ever want to be...

Good... now, while you're relaxing there in the chair, you can just be aware of your body... aware of your hands where they rest on the arms of the chair... perhaps noticing the angle of your elbows and maybe sensing the weight of your head against the chair back... and, you know, that weight might seem to just gently increase as you allow yourself to relax more and more... just being aware of your ankles and feet now, on the footrest, and wondering if they will start to feel heavy too, as you... relax... thinking about your breathing for a few moments... noticing that your breathing is becoming slower and steadier as you relax more and more... slower and steadier... breathing so steadily and evenly... just as though you were pretending to be sound asleep... breathing so evenly, so steadily... you almost wouldn't disturb a feather placed immediately in front of you... breathing so easily and slowly, so gently, that you almost wouldn't disturb even a single strand of a feather placed right in front of you....

And as you allow yourself to relax even more now... I wonder if you can perhaps sense the beating of your own heart... sensing the beat of your own heart and just seeing whether you can use the power of your mind to slow that heartbeat down... just a touch... just seeing whether you can use the power of your mind to slow that heartbeat down just a little... so that you can then feel your whole body slowing down... becoming lazier and lazier... because you've got absolutely nothing whatsoever to do except to relax now... nobody wanting anything, nobody expecting anything... so you can allow your whole body to continue to relax and become steadier and easier until it's just ticking over... like a well maintained machine of some sort or another... just ticking over... smoothly... easily... quietly... comfortably... so that you can become gradually more aware of your whole self... aware of your hands and arms, just sensing how they are now... aware of your legs and feet, too... again just sensing how relaxed they might be, and wondering if it's possible to relax them even more... to be so in touch with yourself that you can actually get your whole body, perhaps, to relax even more... yet remaining totally alert... and noticing now how even your face muscles can begin to really relax... relaxing and letting go of the tensions that were there, almost, but not quite, completely unnoticed... just being vaguely aware of the skin and the muscles of your face settling... smoothing out... a good feeling... wondering just how long all that tension had been there... where it all came from in the first place... and then realising that you simply couldn't care less... because you can feel it draining away from you now... and that feels good... and as you continue to sense the beating of your heart and the absolute steadiness of your body's rhythm... you wonder at the fact that you are so absolutely relaxed and comfortable that you simply can't be bothered to even try to move even one single muscle... even though you know you easily could... if you wanted to... I know that you easily could, if you wanted to... but you simply can't be bothered to even try... allowing yourself to just be... relaxed and relaxing even more now... as lazy and relaxed as anyone could ever wish to be... and I wonder if you can now manage to relax even more... even though you are already as relaxed as it is possible for most people to ever be... just finding the last tiny traces of tension in your body and simply letting them go... with each easy, gentle, breath you breathe... allowing every muscle... every fibre... every cell of your entire body... to be as beautifully relaxed as anyone could ever wish to be...

Now use a deepener if necessary, preferably one which actively features the client.

Method 4

In a moment I'm going to relax you more completely. In a moment I'm going to begin counting backwards from 10 to 1.

The moment I say the number 10 you will allow your eyelids to remain closed. The moment I say the number 10, you will, in your mind's eye, see yourself at the top of a small set of stairs.

The moment I say the number 9, and each additional number, you will simply move down those stairs relaxing more completely. At the base of the stairs is a large feather bed, with a comfortable feather pillow.

The moment I say the number one you will simply sink into that bed, resting your head on that feather pillow.

Number 10, eyes closed at the top of those stairs. Ten ...

Nine, relaxing and letting go. Nine ...

Eight, sinking into a more comfortable, calm, peaceful position.

Seven ....

Six ... going way down ...

Five ... moving down those stairs, relaxing more completely.

Four ...

Three ... breathe in deeply ...

Two ... On the next number, number one, simply sinking into that bed, becoming more calm, more peaceful, more relaxed ...

One ... Sinking into that feather bed, let every muscle go limp and loose as you sink into a more calm, peaceful state of relaxation.

Bibliography

Creating a Bug Free Mind by Andy Shaw

Silence Your Mind by Dr Ramesh Manocha

The Complete Guide to Genius by manifestationintelligence.com

The Millionaire Mindset by Ron G. Holland

Millionaire Secrets by Ron G Holland

Talk and Grow Rich by Ron G Holland

The Millionaire Inside by Paul McCormack

Using a Bug Free Mind by Andy Shaw

Words can change your Brain: Andrew Newberg and Mark Robert Waldman

Printed in Great Britain
by Amazon